Jasmine Baker

Keto Chaffle Recipes

Keto Chaffle Recipes

Learn Quick and Easy Recipes to Prepare Delicious ketogenic Waffles and Lose Weight by Burning Fat and Making your Low-Carb Diet Fun

Jasmine Baker

Table of Contents

Introduction

Nowadays, it seems everyone is talking about the ketogenic (keto) diet - the low-carb, low-protein, high-fat diet that turns your body into a fat-burning machine. Is keto something you should consider? In the following, it is explained what this diet is about, what advantages and disadvantages, and which problems have to be considered.

What is keto?

Usually, the body uses glucose as the main fuel source for energy. If you follow a keto diet and consume very few carbohydrates with moderate amounts of protein (excess protein can be converted into carbohydrates), your body switches the fuel supply so that it is mainly fueled with fat. The liver produces ketones (a sort of unsaturated fat) from fat. These ketones become a wellspring of fuel for the body, especially the psyche, which uses a lot of essentialness and can run on either glucose or ketones.

Benefits of the keto diet

The keto diet is not new. It was used in the 1920s as a medical therapy to treat epilepsy in children. However, until recently, when anti-epileptics came onto the market, nutrition was forgotten. With the success of reducing the number of seizures in epilepsy patients, there is increasing research into whether the diet can treat a range of neurological disorders and other types of chronic diseases.

It can also protect against traumatic brain injuries and strokes.

Type 2 diabetes

Aside from losing weight, the keto diet also helps to increase insulin sensitivity. This is ideal for people with type 2 diabetes. In a study published in Nutrition & Metabolism, the researchers found that diabetics who consumed a low-carbohydrate keto diet could significantly reduce their dependence on diabetes medication and possibly even reverse it. Cancer. Most people are unaware that the main fuel of cancer cells is glucose. That is, eating the correct eating regimen can help stifle malignant growth development. Since the keto diet is low in starches, the disease cells are denied of their fundamental fuel source, the sugar. As ahead of schedule as 1987, examines on keto slims down in various malignant growths indicated diminished tumor development and improved endurance.

Comparison of American, Paleo and Keto diets

(% Of total calorie intake)

Diet Plan	Carbs	Protein	Fat
Standard American Diet	40-60%	15-30%	15-40%
Paleo Diet	20-40%	20-35%	25-50%
Keto Diet	5-10%	10-15%	70-80%

The primary distinction between the keto diet and the standard American or Paleo diet is that it contains significantly fewer sugars and much progressively fat. The keto diet prompts ketosis with flowing ketones in the scope of 0.5 to 5.0 mM. This can be assessed using a home blood ketone meter with ketone test strips. (In the event that it's not all that much difficulty note that ketone testing in pee isn't correct.).

Step by step instructions to figure a keto diet

1. Sugars

To accomplish ketosis (ketones over 0.5 mM), a great many people need to confine sugars to 20 to 50 g/day. The genuine measure of sugars fluctuates from individual to individual. For the most part, the more insulin safe an individual is, the more safe they are to ketosis. Some insulin-touchy competitors who train intensely can devour in excess of 50 g/day and remain in ketosis, while individuals with type 2 diabetes and insulin obstruction should be more like 20-30 g/day.

When figuring starches, you can utilize net starches, i.e. all out carbs short fiber and sugar alcohols. The idea of net starches is to just utilize sugars that increase expansion glucose and insulin. Dietary fiber has no metabolic or hormonal impacts, as do most sugar alcohols. The special case is maltitol, which can significantly affect glucose and insulin. Therefore, if maltitol is on the list of ingredients, sugar alcohol should not be subtracted from the total carbohydrates.

The amount of carbohydrates that can be consumed and that remains in ketosis can also change over time, depending on the keto adjustment, weight loss, exercise habits, medication, etc. Therefore, you should routinely measure your ketone levels.

In terms of general nutrition, carbohydrate-rich foods such as pasta, muesli, potatoes, rice, beans, sugary sweets, lemonades, juices, and lager are not reasonable.

Most dairy items contain starches as lactose (milk sugar). Notwithstanding, some have less starches and can be utilized consistently. These incorporate hard cheddar (Parmesan, Cheddar), delicate, high-fat cheddar (Brie), high-fat cream cheddar, overwhelming whipped cream, and sharp cream.

A sugar substance of under 50 g/day is commonly made up as follows:

5-10 g carbohydrates from protein foods. Eggs, cheese, and shellfish contain a few grams of carbohydrates from natural sources, as well as marinades and spices.

10-15 g carbohydrates from non-starchy vegetables.

5-10 g of starches from nuts/seeds. Most nuts contain 5-6 g of starches for every ounce.

5-10 g of starches from natural products, for example, berries, olives, tomatoes, and avocados.

5-10 g of starches from different sources, for example, low-carb pastries, high-fat dressings, or beverages with exceptionally low measures of sugar.

refreshments

A great many people need in any event a large portion of a gallon of all-out liquid daily. The best sources are sifted water, natural espresso, and tea (typical and without sugar, unsweetened) just as unsweetened almond and coconut milk. Diet soft drinks and beverages ought to be maintained a strategic distance from as they contain fake sugars. In the event that you drink red or white wine, confine yourself to 1-2 glasses. The drier, the better. In the event that you drink spirits, maintain a strategic distance from the improved blended beverages.

2. Protein

A keto diet is anything but a high protein diet. This is on the grounds that protein expands insulin and can be changed over to glucose through a procedure called gluconeogenesis, which represses ketosis. Nonetheless, a keto diet ought not to be excessively low in protein either, as this can bring about loss of muscle tissue and capacity.

It is important that the calculation is based on lean body mass and not total body weight. The reason for this is that to maintain fat mass, no protein is required, only muscle mass.

For example, if a person weighs 150 lbs (or 150 / 2.2 = 68.18 kg) and has a body fat content of 20% (or a lean body mass of 80% = 68.18 kg × 0.8 = 54.55 kg) , the protein requirement can vary from 44 (= 54.55 × 0.8) to 82 (= 54.55 × 1.5) g / day.

The upper limit applies to those who are very active or athletic. For anyone else who uses the keto diet for weight loss or other health benefits, the daily amount of protein can be somewhere in between.

Best sources of high-quality protein are:

Organic pastured eggs (6-8 g protein/egg)

Grass-fed meat (6-9 g protein/oz)

Animal sources of omega-3 fats such as wild-caught Alaska salmon, sardines, anchovies, and herring. (6-9 g protein / ounce)

Nuts and seeds, for example, macadamia, almonds, walnuts, flax, hemp and sesame. (4-8 g protein/quarter cup)

Vegetables (1-2 g protein/oz)

3. Fat

After we discover the definite measures of starches and protein, the remainder of the eating routine originates from fat. A keto diet is fundamentally high in fat. If enough fat is eaten, the bodyweight is maintained.

For people who consume 2,000 calories a day to maintain their weight, the daily fat intake is between 156 and 178 g / day. In large or very active people with high energy requirements who keep their weight, the fat intake can even exceed 300 g / day.

Most people can tolerate high fat intake, but certain conditions such as gallbladder removal can affect the amount of fat that can be consumed in a single meal. In this case, more frequent meals or the use of bile salts or pancreatic enzymes with a high lipase content can be helpful.

Avoid unwanted fats such as trans fats, highly refined polyunsaturated vegetable oils, and large amounts of polyunsaturated omega-6 fatty acids.

The best foods to get high-quality fats include:

Avocados and Avocado Oil

Coconuts and coconut oil

Grass-fed butter, ghee, and beef fat

Organic cream in the pasture

olive oil

Pig fat from grazing pigs

Medium-chain triglycerides (MCTs)

MCT is a special type of fat that is metabolized differently than normal long-chain fatty acids. With the help of MCTs, the liver can quickly produce energy even before glucose increases the production of ketones.

Concentrated MCT oil sources are available as a supplement. Many people use it to achieve ketosis. The main nourishment that is particularly high in MCTs is coconut oil. Around 66% of the coconut fat originates from MCT.

Who ought to be cautious with a keto diet?

For the vast majority, a keto diet is extremely sheltered. In any case, there are a few people who need to take a unique mind and talk about with their primary care physicians before following such an eating regimen.

The individuals who take drugs for diabetes: The measurement should be balanced as the glucose diminishes with a low-carb diet.

The individuals who take drugs for hypertension: Measurements should be balanced if pulse drops with a low-carb diet.

The individuals who are breastfeeding ought not to follow an exceptionally severe low-carb diet, as the body can lose around 30 g of sugars for every day through milk. In this manner, take in any event 50 g of sugars for every day during breastfeeding.

Patients with kidney sickness ought to counsel their primary care physician before beginning a keto diet.

Basic worries about a keto diet

Can't accomplish ketosis. Ensure you don't eat an excessive amount of protein and that the bundled nourishments don't contain shrouded starches.

Eat inappropriate kinds of fat like the profoundly refined polyunsaturated corn and soybean oils.

Manifestations of keto influenza incorporate languor, discombobulation, migraine, exhaustion, mind mist, and obstruction. With ketosis, the body will, in general, discharge more sodium. If you don't get enough sodium from your eating routine, you may encounter side effects of keto influenza. The cure is 2 cups of juices (with included salt) every day. In the event that you practice energetically or the perspiration rate is high, you may need to include more sodium.

Daybreak impact. Ordinary fasting glucose is beneath 100 mg/dl, and most ketosis patients arrive at this level on the off chance that they are not diabetic. In certain individuals, in any case, fasting glucose will, in general, increment, particularly toward the beginning of the day in the event that you are on a keto diet. This is known as the "first light impact" and is because of the ordinary circadian increment in morning cortisol (stress hormone), which animates the liver to deliver more glucose. For this situation, ensure that you are not eating an excessive amount of protein at supper and are not very short before hitting the hay. Stress and poor rest can likewise prompt higher cortisol levels. In case you're insulin safe, you may likewise require more opportunity to get ketosis.

Low athletic performance. The keto adjustment usually takes about 4 weeks. Meanwhile, switch to something that is less vigorous instead of doing intense workouts or workouts. After the adjustment phase, athletic performance usually returns to normal or even better, especially in endurance sports.

Keto rash is not a common side effect of the diet. Possible causes include the formation of acetone (a form of ketone) in the sweat that irritates the skin, or nutritional deficiencies, including protein or minerals. Scrub down following your exercise and ensure you eat nutritious entire nourishments.

Ketoacidosis. This is an exceptionally uncommon condition that happens when the blood ketone level is over 15 mM. A well-detailed keto diet doesn't cause ketoacidosis. Certain ailments, for example, type 1 diabetes, prescription with SGLT-2 inhibitors for type 2 diabetes, or breastfeeding, require an uncommon alert. Indications incorporate laziness, queasiness, retching, and fast, shallow relaxation. Gentle cases can be helped with sodium bicarbonate blended in with the weakened orange or squeezed apple. Serious symptoms require immediate medical attention.

Is keto safe in the long term?

This is an area that is controversial. Although there have been no studies indicating harmful long-term effects of a keto diet, many experts now believe that if one does not enter and exit regularly, the body may develop "resistance" to the benefits of ketosis. In addition, a long-term high-fat diet may not be suitable for all body types.

Cyclical keto diet

Once you are able to consistently produce more than 0.5 mM ketones in the blood, it is time to get the carbohydrates back into your diet. Instead of eating only 20-50 g of carbohydrates a day, you can increase them to 100-150 g on these days. As a rule, 2-3 times a week is sufficient. Ideally, this also happens on strength training days when you actually increase your protein intake.

This approach to cycling can make the eating plan more acceptable to some people who refuse to permanently eliminate some of their favorite foods. However, it can also degrade determination and commitment to the keto diet or lead to binges in susceptible individuals.

Chapter 1.   Keto Diet Explained

There are many diets gaining traction today, but none like the ketogenic diet. However, the interesting thing about this diet is that it is not used for weight loss. For the past century, it has been used as a way to treat epilepsy. However, because this diet is so temperamental, this is only done with the strictest doctor supervision. The ketogenic diet is a diet that is designed to release ketones in your bloodstream. Many of the cells in your body prefer to use blood sugar, which it gets from carbohydrates, as your body's main source of energy. The idea of the ketogenic diet is to put your body in a state of ketosis.

A warning that this book will give you before we proceed is that the ketogenic diet is not considered to be safe. Doctors all over the world and from the most prestigious medical practices advise against it for a few reasons. The first being that this diet was only invented to help people in the most extreme situations and even then not forever.

Doctors recommend this diet for no longer than six months and even then only under constant contact and supervision by a doctor that you see. It has also been shown to put certain people into a state called ketoacidosis, which can be fatal. This is especially true in diabetics. They could die in under an hour. It can also worsen those with kidney disease as well as making you have sleep problems and stomach issues along with constipation and vomiting. Another downside is this diet has been shown to be heavy on red meat and other processed foods that are salty and fatty, which is unhealthy. You should also avoid keto if your pregnant as it could harm your unborn child as well as yourself.

The next is the high protein diet. This one is similar to the basic diet, but obviously, it will include more protein. The numbers that this diet offers is 5% carbs, 35% protein, and 60% fat.

The third is the cyclical diet. This diet involves what is known as refeeding. The basis for this diet is that you have periods of higher-carb refeeds. For example, you have five ketogenic diet days and then two high carb days.

The last diet is the basic diet. This is the one that is used most often and by most people. The numbers for this one are as follows, 75% fat with only 5% carbs and 20% protein.

It is worth noting that the only two diets that have been studied extensively are the basic and high protein diet. The other two are more advanced, and bodybuilders and athletes are the ones that generally use them, although it's not ideal or recommended since they need further study.

The ketogenic diet believes that it is an effective way to lose weight and help lower your risk factors for disease. It is also believed to be filling, and you can lose weight without having to count your calories or track what you're eating. However, this isn't true. The ketogenic diet makes you track your food very carefully because you need to know where your fat and carbs are, as well as the protein content. If you're not tracking these things, you could throw yourself out of where you are supposed to be.

Another benefit is that it is believed that it can help with diabetes. This is because it can help you lose excess fat, which is very closely related to diabetes. Especially in type 2 diabetes. One study found that it can improve insulin sensitivity by 75%. However, this should be looked into more as other studies have found problems with this diet. Another belief is that it can help with cancer, Alzheimer's disease, and heart disease.

We have already mentioned that it has been used to treat epilepsy, but it is also said that it can help with polycystic ovary syndrome or PCS for short as well as Parkinson's disease. Brain injuries have been studied in one animal study, but there is much more research that is needed to be conclusive. On the lower scale, it may be able to help with acne as well.

The keto diet will set up your body to deplete the stored glucose. Once that is accomplished, your body will focus on diminishing the stored fat you have saved as fuel. Many people don't understand that counting calories don't matter at this point since it is just used as a baseline. Your body doesn't need glucose which will trigger these two stages:

The State of Glycogenesis: The excess of glucose converts itself into glycogen, which is stored in the muscles and liver. Research indicates that only about half of your energy used daily can be saved as glycogen.

The State of Lipogenesis: This phase is introduced when there is an adequate supply of glycogen in your liver and muscles, with any excess being converted to fat and stored.

When the glycerol and fatty acid molecules are released, the ketogenesis process begins, and acetoacetate is produced. The Acetoacetate is converted to two types of ketone units:

Acetone: This is mostly excreted as waste but can also be metabolized into glucose. This is the reason individuals on a ketogenic diet will experience a distinctive smelly breath.

Beta-hydroxybutyrate or BHB: Your muscles will convert the acetoacetate into BHB, which will fuel your brain after you have been on the keto diet for a short time.

There are many foods that you can eat on this diet, but there are many foods that you can't, and its this subject, in particular, that we're going to go into now. The following foods that you need to avoid eating are the following.

• Fruit- You will need to avoid all fruits except small portions of certain kinds like berries.

• Beans- Peas and beans like kidney beans are to be avoided as well because they are too high in carbs.

• Legumes- Lentils will also need to be avoided.

• Starches and grains - Wheat products like pasta and cereal are a big no-no, and you will have to stay away from these as well.

• Sugary foods- fruit juice, smoothies, junk food, and things like ice cream and cake are out as well.

- Sugar -free foods- These are most often found in sugar alcohols or diet foods that claim to help you lose weight. They are very highly processed, and they can affect your ketone levels in a negative way.

- Alcohol- The carb content on these is very high, and they can knock you out of where you need to be.

- Root vegetables or tubers- This category means potatoes (including sweet potatoes) and things like carrots.

- Unhealthy fats- You should seriously limit your intake of the fats that are processed. This includes mayonnaise and vegetable oil.

- Diet items and low-fat items- These are overloaded with carbs and are extremely processed.

- Condiments and sauces- They contain too much sugar and fat that is unhealthy.

The foods that you should eat on this diet to make sure that you are following it correctly are the following. As we have stated above, some of these foods are unhealthy such as forms of coconut oil and red meats.

- Healthy oils- The three main ones to focus on are avocado oil, extra virgin olive oil, and coconut oil.

- Cheese- You can eat many different varieties, such as mozzarella, cheddar, cream, or blue. You should go for unprocessed cheeses.

- Eggs- Look for omega-3 whole eggs or pastured eggs.

- Fatty fish-Salmon, tuna, mackerel, and trout are all good options for you.

- Meat-Turkey, bacon, chicken, and sausage are all good options. Red meat and steak are other options as well.

- Butter-Try and get grass-fed if you can.

- Cream- As with butter, if you can find grass-fed, then go for that.

- Nuts-Almonds and walnuts are great options here.

- Seeds-Pumpkin seeds, flax seeds, and chia seeds are all good options, but a warning is that many seeds can cause issues with your digestion and stomach.

- Low carb vegetables- Most green vegetables are alright, and you can have peppers, onions, and tomatoes as well.

- Avocados- You can use them for guacamole, or you can eat them whole. Whole avocados can be used for so many recipes.

- Spices- You can use herbs and spices (healthy ones) and salt and pepper in moderation, of course.

Other healthy foods that you can eat as long as you are careful because the numbers vary as far as carbs (though most are zero and others go as high as 7 grams).

- Lamb

- Jerky

- Veal

- Bison

- Venison

- Sardines

- Shellfish (careful on this one the carbs will add up)

- Catfish

- Cod

- Herring

- Lobster

- Haddock

- Broccoli

- Cauliflower

- Brussels sprouts

- Kale

- Eggplant

- Asparagus

- Cucumber

- Mushrooms

- Green beans

- Celery

- Spinach

- Cabbage

- Swiss chard

- Zucchini

- Olives

- Strawberries

- Grapefruit (be careful on this one the carbs can get really high very quickly)

- Apricots

- Lemons

- Kiwis

- Mulberries

- Oranges

- Raspberries

- Peanuts

- Sunflower seeds

- Pistachios

- Macadamia nuts

- Hazelnuts

- Cashews

- Coconuts

- Full fat yogurt

- Greek yogurt

- Lard

- Tallow

- Coffee

- Tea

- Carbonated water

- Club soda

- Dark chocolate (choose real dark chocolate with 70 percent cocoa at least)

Food is such an important part of this diet that it's important to make sure that you're informed on it so that you can have the best knowledge and the knowledge that is going to be of the most useful to you. Having the right information means you can be successful; having the wrong information can lead to injuries or worse. Doctors have said that you should always ask them before starting this diet at all, but this is proven to be more true if you have the following health issues.

- Obesity

- Heart conditions

- High blood pressure

- Diabetes

- Kidney issues

- Cancer

- Epilepsy

The reason that you should have their supervision is that these are all serious conditions. Especially things like cancer and epilepsy.

Exercise is so important on this diet as well, and it is important to understand how you need to utilize it for your benefit. Exercise is important in any diet that you choose, and it's important to be able to understand that exercise is what you need to become a healthier person, but it can actually be harder on the keto diet because your body is being put through so much already.

As such, your routine is going to change. The main reason is that your not using carbs for energy and fuel, your using fat for fuel. Fat doesn't give you that energy burst that you need for push-ups or jumps like carbs do. You will probably not feel like working out at all because of how your feelings, but you will be able to get past this, and you will be able to make a good routine for yourself.

Because workouts like sprinting, weightlifting, and high-intensity interval training are workouts all require that quick burst of energy, they are going to be much more strenuous though many say it won't be impossible. Just remember the reason for this is because the fat in your body is not as available to your muscles as the energy that you get from carbs are. Because of this, you are more likely to get tired during these workouts and much quicker than you usually do.

This doesn't mean you have to stop working out; it means you have to be smarter about how you work out. Jogging and bike riding are both great options for you to do on this diet, and a good rule of thumb is to go for something that is low to moderate as far as your workout and do something for a short duration. This is especially true for the first two weeks that you start this. With your doctor's permission, you can talk to them about going into higher amounts of workout, but you need to have their help with this, so check with them first.

If your feeling drained on the basic diet, another option is to try the targeted diet or the cyclical diet. This is not recommended for a lot of people, so this would be another area where you need to check with your doctor as well to see if this is alright for you. Another issue with doing this is that you will knock yourself out of that ketosis state that they want you to stay in. Overall, it has been proven that working out doesn't feel as good on the keto diet as it did before. This is another reason that the keto diet isn't for everyone. If you love exercising, this isn't the best choice for you. This is especially true because exercise is important for health.

It is recommended that, along with speaking to your doctor about what exercises are good for you to do for yourself, is to speak to a nutritionist professional and a certified trainer as well. This will make sure that you have a great workout plan that is safe. You should also not do any workouts that you haven't done before. This is because this diet can affect how that workout is going to affect you, and the result could be very negative. Other tips that you need to be aware of is that when your working out on this diet are the following tips.

Listen to your body and what it's telling you. You should never keep going or pushing if your body is telling you it can't do it or handle it. If your body is telling you to stop, then you need to stop. Feelings of dizziness and exhaustion or even just fatigue are all signs that you should stop. They are not normal, and this is a sign that your body isn't responding well to this diet and that you need a doctor's help.

Make sure that you are eating enough. This is another big thing with this diet, and this doesn't just include keeping your calorie count where it needs to be. This means keeping your fat where it needs to be, as well. Remember that when your exercising, your body normally uses carbs than fat. Now your using fat. So if you're not taking in enough nutrition, you are not going to be able to handle even the simplest workout. You could actually be putting yourself in danger.

Avoid high-intensity workouts. This is so important with the keto diet. More is not better. In many cases, this is something that is true. The keto diet is considered to be an extreme diet, and as such, you won't be able to do what you are normally able to do. You have to be able to understand that high-intensity workouts are something that is no longer going to be able for you to do. Instead, remember that you really need to stick to a lower intensity workout instead. This is really important particularly important when your starting this diet and for at least the first month that you're doing this.

This diet puts a lot of stress on your body, and it can take a very long time to adjust if your actually able to adjust at all. Many people can't, and this is something to be aware of when you try. Don't push yourself too hard on this diet, or you will end up hurting yourself. If you pace yourself and eat well, you may be able to adjust and lose weight.

Some lower intensity ideas for working out when you're doing the keto diet are the following.

- Rowing

- Hiking

Gymnastics is also good for preventing injury and improving flexibility as well as improving how you move.

An example of a low-intensity workout that you can do is walking. This is easy to do, and it is great for losing weight. Swimming is another good activity though it straddles the fence. If you go lightly and keep it in the low-intensity area, then you are alright. If you push too hard, it could be dangerous. When you are able to keep this thought in mind, you will be able to perform exercises safely and make sure that they are working for you, not against you.

Tips for Success

Routines are very important on this diet, and it's something that will help you stay healthy. As such, in this chapter, we are going to be giving you tips and tricks to make this diet work better for you and help you get an idea of routines that you can put in place for yourself.

Tip number one that is so important is DRINK WATER! This is absolutely vital for any diet that your on, and you need it if not on one as well. However, this vital tip is crucial on a keto diet because when you are eating fewer carbs, you are storing less water, meaning that you are going to get dehydrated very easily. You should aim for more than the daily amount of water; however, remember that drinking too much water can be fatal as your kidneys can only handle so much as once. While this has mostly happened to soldiers in the military, it does happen to dieters as well, so it is something to be aware of.

Chapter 2. The Meaning of Chaffle

Chaffles (short for cheddar waffles) are the most recent famous nourishment in the keto world. It's nothing unexpected — the chaffle has a great deal putting it all on the line. This straightforward keto formula is fresh, brilliant dark-colored, sans sugar, low-carb, and exceptionally simple to make.

A chaffle, or cheddar waffle, is a keto waffle made with eggs and cheddar. Chaffles are turning into an extremely well-known keto/low-carb nibble.

A chaffle is a waffle yet made with a cheddar base. Basically, it's an obliterated cheddar and an egg mix. Once in for a short time for logically fluffier recipes, it's a cream cheddar base instead of decimated cheddar. It's the a la mode new keto-pleasing bread since it's low in carbs, and it won't spike your insulin levels, causing fat accumulating.

The fundamentals are some combo of egg and cheddar; however, from here, you can riff like wild-eyed. You can use an arrangement of cheeses, including cream cheddar, parmesan cheddar, etc. Some incorporate almond flour and flaxseed and getting ready powder, and others don't.

The major recipe for a chaffle contains cheddar, almond flour, and an egg. You consolidate the fixings in an astonish and pour it your waffle maker. Waffle makers are no doubt on the rising right now after this chaffle recipe exploded a couple of days back earlier. I was, to some degree, suspicious from the beginning intuition there was no possibility this would turn out in the wake of joining everything and pouring the hitter over the waffle. Try to sprinkle the waffle maker really well. The waffle wound up exceptional, and it was firm apparently and fragile in the inside.

You can concoct a chaffle utilizing a waffle iron or smaller than usual waffle producer. The cook time is just a couple of moments, and on the off chance that you cook the chaffle right, you end up with a fresh, gooey, flavorful bread/waffle elective.

Chaffles are turning into somewhat of a furor with supporters of the keto diet. They're less fastidious about making than most keto bread recipes, and they're anything but difficult to customize. You can transform the fundamental formula for a chaffle into your own creation, running from flavorful to sweet and anything in the middle. You can likewise change the sort of cheddar you use, delivering significant changes in the flavor and surface of the chaffle. Cheddar and mozzarella cheddar are the two most regular decisions, yet you can likewise include parmesan, cream cheddar, or whatever other cheddar that melts well.

The most fundamental clarification of a Chaffle is that it's an extraordinary bread elective when on the keto diet. It copies the vibe of a waffle; however, Keto clients have been utilizing Chaffles in a wide range of recipes from sandwiches to sweets. There are a huge amount of Keto Chaffle Recipes out there.

It's made with cheddar, so get it? At the point when you work cheddar and waffle —
you get chaffle (and you additionally get enchantment.) Well enough with the back
story. Since you realize what this keto nourishment is, how about we make one and let
you see with your own eyes how astounding this keto waffle is.

WHAT IS NEEDED TO PREPARE A CHAFFLE

• 1 tremendous egg

• 1/2 c. Cheddar

• 2 tablespoons of almond flour

HOW TO PREPARE A CHAFFLE

There are a few hints, techniques, and approaches you'll need to know to make your
chaffles particularly fresh.

Most importantly, don't eat your chaffles directly out of the waffle iron. They'll be wet
and eggy from the outset, however on the off chance that you let them sit for 3-4
minutes, they'll be fresh right up.

Second, for extra fresh chaffles, you can include an additional layer of destroyed
cheddar (or another cheddar that gets firm, similar to parmesan) to the two sides of
the waffle producer's surface. Set out the destroyed cheddar, pour in the hitter, put
more cheddar on top, and afterward cook the chaffle typically. You'll wind up with a
firm, sautéed bits of cheddar installed in the outside of the chaffle.

Everyone is going looney tunes, asking, "How might I make these?!" This is the game
plan. The principal recipe on what and how. The fundamental equation consolidates
crushed cheddar and an egg; however, there are tremendous measures of add-ins you

can use to change the flavor! You will make a direct chaffle hitter and cook it in a waffle maker!

THE WAFFLE TOOLS TO MAKE EASY KETO CHAFFLES

A standard waffle creator will deliver a chaffle that appears as though the universally adored round solidified toaster waffles, which is flawless as keto bread for sandwiches, a bun for burgers, or even a shell for tacos. One famous brand is the Dash smaller than expected waffle creator, which is entirely reasonable and makes slender, fresh chaffles.

A Belgian waffle creator makes thicker waffles with profound scores. That is incredible for typical waffle-production; however, it isn't perfect for chaffles. They end up less fresh, with a greater amount of an omelet-like consistency. Your most logical option is to get a standard waffle producer.

HOW TO EAT CHAFFLES

There are a lot of famous approaches to eat chaffles:

- Plain. Chaffles are incredible, all alone as a morning meal nourishment. You can serve them up close by bacon, eggs, avocado, and other standard keto breakfast passage.
- Keto chaffle sandwich. Make two chaffles and use them as bread for your preferred sandwich. Chaffles are extraordinary as the bread for BLTs, turkey clubs, breakfast sandwiches, or some other keto-accommodating sandwich.
- Chaffle dessert. Attempt one of the sweet chaffle varieties recorded underneath and present with keto maple syrup or your most loved keto frozen yogurt.

THE DIFFERENT TYPE OF WAFFLE MAKER NEEDED TO MAKE A CHAFFLE

By far, most genuinely like to use a Dash Mini Waffle Maker; however, you can use any waffle maker you have. There is a wide scope of waffle makers. Honestly, you, in all likelihood, have one in the back of your kitchen organizers that you haven't used in quite a while.

THE VARIOUS TYPES OF BASIC KETO CHAFFLE RECIPES

Keto Chaffle Recipes eBook Cookbook for beginners 2020, includes delicious and appealing keto recipes for each flavor palette.

1. Basic Chaffle Recipes
2. Savory Chaffle Recipes
3. Sweet Chaffle Recipes
4. Chaffle Cake Recipes

Various Cheeses

Cheddar, mozzarella, parmesan, cream cheddar, Colby jack — any cheddar that melts well will work with a chaffle. Distinctive cheddar produces various flavors and somewhat various surfaces. Attempt a couple and locate your top choice.

Sweet Chaffles

Utilize a nonpartisan cheddar like mozzarella or cream cheddar. At that point, include a touch of your most loved keto sugar to the hitter before you cook it. You can likewise chocolate chips or low-sugar fruits like blueberries or strawberries. Top with keto frozen yogurt or keto whipped cream for a delectable chaffle dessert.

Exquisite Chaffles

Include exquisite fixings like herbs and flavors to your chaffle. For a pizza chaffle, include oregano, garlic powder, and diced pepperoni in the hitter, with tomato sauce and additional cheddar on top. Or on the other hand, you could utilize cream cheddar and add everything bagel flavoring to the player for an everything bagel chaffle. Present with more cream cheddar on top, tricks, onions, and smoked salmon.

RULES ON HOW TO MAKE THE BEST CHAFFLES

1.   Layering. In the event that you're making a chaffle with cheddar, the best way to deal with do this is to layer cheddar at the base, pour in a tablespoon or so of egg, and a short time later top with cheddar again. It's the firm cheddar on the base and top that will make them new.

2.   Shallow waffles. If you need new waffles, the shallower the waffle iron, the more straightforward/faster it is to new up the chaffle.

3.   No over-burdening. Stuffed chaffle makers... well, they flood clearly, which makes colossal destruction! So when in doubt, underfill rather than pressing. Near 1/4 cup of TOTAL fixings in a steady progression.

4.   Crush it. I've thought about others using press bottles so they can get just a little egg into the small scale waffle maker.

5.   Simple cleanup. I like to use a wet paper towel when the waffle iron is warm, to make cleanup straightforward. Not hot, however, obviously! Essentially warm.

6.   Brush it. I've found toothbrush works outstandingly to clean between the waffle iron teeth. You can, in like manner, endeavor this wipe cleaner, which I also use to clean the little region on the edge of my Instant Pot.

7.   No looking. I can tell you from LOTS of individual experience, that opening the waffle iron at normal interims "just to check" doesn't hep the chaffle cook any speedier. Your most consistent choice is to not using any and all means open it for 4-5 minutes.

8.   Get hot. Hold up until the waffle iron is hot before you incorporate fixings, and they're essentially less slanted to adhere and a lot easier to clean up.

9.   Cut or shred. I understand most recipes out there suggest demolished cheddar, yet I have better karma with the slimmest cut of cheddar I can buy. I find it crisps essentially speedier.

10.   Not really gooey. In case you need them to taste less gooey, endeavor mozzarella cheddar.

11.   Fresh Cooling. License the chaffles to cool before eating. They get crisper as they cool, so take the necessary steps not to stuff the hot chaffle into your mouth right away.

12.   Make parts. Make enough to share, and everyone will require them, whether or not they're keto or not.

Chaffles Nutrition and Carb Count

You'll get two chaffles out of an enormous egg and about a large portion of a cup of cheddar. Contingent upon the cheddar you use, your calories and net carb check will change a tad. Yet, as a rule, expecting you utilize genuine, entire milk cheddar like cheddar or mozzarella (rather than cream cheddar or American cheddar), chaffles are totally sans carb. A normal serving size of two chaffles contains generally:

- 300 calories
- 0g all out carbs
- 0g net carbs
- 20g protein
- 23g fat

As should be obvious, chaffles are about as keto as a formula can be: high-fat, high-protein, and zero-carb. They even work on the flesh-eater diet, if you eat cheddar.

Chapter 3. Why Keto Chaffles Are Popular

Why chaffles and not waffles? Chaffles are waffles that are made of eggs and cheese, with the latter ingredient being their base. You can, however, also add a few other ingredients to suit your preference and to get the most nutrition out of your chaffle. In fact, there are so many variations to this low-carb waffles that you can literally have a different chaffle recipe for every mood and occasion.

The main difference between a waffle and a chaffle is that instead of using cheese like chaffles, waffles use flour as their base ingredient. This means that chaffles do not contain as many carbs as waffles, with most containing below 5g. As such, if you are on a keto diet or you simply want to minimize your carbs intake while still enjoying your delicious snacks, then chaffles is the way to go. In addition, chaffles contain sufficient fat to ensure you attain the required level of macronutrients in your diet.

As we have already seen, the base ingredient for chaffles is cheese, and these come in a wide variety. This makes it easy for you to produce varied chaffle recipes that bring out varying texture and flavors.

The type of cheese you decide to use could be influenced by personal preference, availability of the cheese, or other different factors. Some of the common cheeses you can use to give chaffles their texture and shape include mozzarella cheese, cheddar cheese, Colby jack cheese, cream cheese, parmesan cheese, and others. It is important to note that cheese that is finely shredded will give you a finer taste compared to those that are thickly shredded, but you can test with different sizes of shreds and see what works best for you.

As you will also see in the recipes provided in this book, there is a vast range of ingredients you can use as chaffle toppings, which include kewpie mayonnaise, green onion, and bonito flakes. Spices such as garlic powder and black pepper can also be used to spice up your chaffle toppings.

You can also use different sauces such as soy sauce, pasta sauce, ketchup, and Worcestershire sauce to accompany your chaffles and enhance their individual tastes. Different vegetables such as lettuce, tomato, and cauliflower are also used to go along with your chaffles to ensure the chaffle meals you consume are not only filling but also nutritious.

You now probably want to try and make some chaffles, but you do not know where to start. Well, luckily, chaffles do not take up much time to prepare or even cook. Most recipes actually take just 4 to 6 steps, as you will soon see. Most include mixing the ingredients together, pouring the batter onto the waffle plate, and cooking for a few minutes with only a few variations to suit the different recipes. In about 5 to 20 minutes, you should be done depending on the number of chaffles you opt to make.

Making chaffles does not also call for fancy tools, yet you will be able to make some quick and nutritious chaffles. All you need is measuring cups, a few mixing bowls, wooden spoons or spatulas, and a waffle maker, and that is it! Some people even prefer to make the batter into pancakes by pouring the batter onto a pan instead of a waffle maker, and it works just as well. If you do not have access to a waffle maker, you can decide to use the latter option.

The beauty of chaffles is that you can store them for up to 7 days so you can enjoy them throughout the week. To preserve, simply wrap your chaffles tightly in a parchment paper then put them in a stasher or zip-lock bag and place in the refrigerator. When it's time to consume, all you have to do is take the chaffles out of the storage bag, let them thaw, then toast them using a toaster. Another way to reheat them is to wrap a paper towel around them and place them in a microwave for 30 to 60 seconds.

Chaffles can be enjoyed at any time of the day. You can have them in the morning as a healthy breakfast option, at lunchtime as an alternative to sandwich buns, or even at dinner where they can become a base for your dinner toppings. You can also snack on chaffles in between meals when you feel hungry instead of going for unhealthy snacks. They are also light and easy to carry around, so you can carry some to work or school for a quick and convenient snack option.

Chapter 4. Frequently Asked Questions (Faq)

A few questions about chaffles are frequently asked here. Here are responses to some of the most popular ketogenic diet-related questions.

DOES CHAFFLE TASTE LIKE EGGS AND CHEESE?

Yes ... no ... And it's hard to answer because we all have different flavors. I think this is the best thing I can offer you ... if I personally offered you a waffle chaffle with syrup, you would think you were eating a waffle.

If you served a delicious waffle as sandwich bread, you would think that making a sandwich in a waffle would be a bit strange, but you wouldn't think it tasted like egg and cheese.

But, however ... but it all depends on the ingredients you use and the flavors you add. There were many ideas that this recipe could be played in different ways, but it was overwhelming.

Most importantly, if you are using waffles as a sandwich shell, the sandwich stuffing will be the star of the show. These flavors are located at the front and center, and the chaffle flavors are located at the rear seats. Does it make sense?

WHAT IS THE BEST CHEESE TO MAKE CHAFFLE?

Oh, another interesting question. Today, we usually use classic, neutral flavors. The choice of cheese actually depends on the flavor. If you're making low carb bread, you want to chaffle the ancillary actors instead of the reeds.

So the best cheese for that is Mozzarella cheese. I like to use finely ground ones. Because it mixes a little better with the egg, and I generally like to shred my cheese, but the pre-shreds work very well here and add to the useful factors.

Yes, you can use many other cheeses, but if you want the cheese to shine, you should. The world is your oyster! Enjoy! And experiment!

AM I GOING TO LOSE MY MUSCLE?

There is a possibility that any diet will lose any muscle. Nevertheless, a high intake of protein and high levels of ketone can help to reduce muscle loss, particularly when lifting weights.

CAN I USE A KETOGENIC DIET TO BUILD MUSCLE?

Yes, but a moderate-carb diet may not perform as well. Read this article for more information on low-carb diets and exercise efficiency.

DO I NEED CARBURIZATION OR REFEED?

No. No. No. Nonetheless, every now and then, a couple of higher-calorie days may be helpful.

WHAT IF I'M TIRED, WEAK OR TIRED AT ALL TIMES?

You may not be in full ketosis to make efficient use of fats and ketones. To counter this, raising the consumption of carb and review the above points, It may also help a supplement such as MCT oil or ketones.

MY PEE HAS A FRUITY SCENT. WHY IS IT?

Don't worry. This is simply due to the excretion during ketosis of by-products.

The scent of the air. What am I going to do?

It's a common side effect. Try to drink flavored water naturally or to chew sugar-free gum.

I READ THAT KETOSIS WAS VERY RISKY. IS IT TRUE?

Ketosis is often associated with ketoacidosis by men. The former is normal, whereas, in uncontrolled diabetes, the latter happens only.

Ketoacidosis is risky, but it is perfectly normal and healthy to have ketogenic diet ketosis.

That's true. I'm having problems with digestion and diarrhea. What am I going to do?

Generally, after 3–4 weeks, this common side effect disappears. If it continues, try to eat more vegetables of high fiber. Constipation can also be helped by magnesium supplements.

DO YOU JUST TASTE CHAFFLES LIKE EGGS AND CHEESE?

While plain chaffles can taste like eggs and cheese, with just about any flavor, you can customize chaffles. Using a mild cheese such as mozzarella can eliminate much of the taste of cheese and eggs, leaving you with a blank canvas to fill up as you see fit.

WHY STUCK THE CHAFFLE ON THE GRILL AND CONFUSED IT A BIT?

This happens when the griddle does not cook a long enough chaffle. The dough is not completely cooked before lifting or trying to remove it, and the dough remains stuck to the outside when the griddle is opened. I think it's best to cook most chaffle recipes for at least 3-4 minutes.

A simple dough with cream cheese, eggs, and cheese can get away in at least 3 minutes. In some cases, if the recipe contains chicken or tuna, it will need to be cooked longer. Cooking time for protein-based chaffles is 4-7 minutes, depending on the recipe.

WHY STICK THE STICK ON THE GRILL AND CAUSE STICKY CONFUSION

You don't cook your chaffle with griddle long enough; I know this will happen. If you lift or remove the dough and then remove it, the dough will not be fully cooked and will separate and stick out when the grid is opened.

It is recommended to cook a chaffle recipe for at least 3-4 minutes. For basic cream cheese, eggs, and cheese dough, you can get away in at least 3 minutes. In some cases, if chicken or tuna are included in the recipe, they need to be cooked longer. Based on the recipe, the cooking time for protein-based chaffles is 4-7 minutes.

WITHOUT A WAFFLE MAKER, WOULD YOU MAKE CHAFFLES

Without a waffle iron, it's hard to get the crispiness of the chaffles. That said, in a pan that holds a lot of heat, like a cast iron, you should try to mix up the chaffle batter and cook it like a pancake. You probably won't end up with a perfect, standardized end result, but it's still going to be pretty good.

CAN YOU USE CHAFFLES TO FREEZE

You will freeze up to a month's chaffles. Defrosting them, though, adds a lot of moisture, making it hard to get them crisp again. Because they're so fast and easy to produce (the overall cooking time is less than 10 minutes), you're probably better off making up a fresh batch whenever you're feeling like a chaffle.

CAN YOU HEAT UP CHAFFLES

If you are planning to make and reheat the chaffles in advance, you might want to invest in an air fryer. Once they have been in a fridge or freezer, it can be difficult to get chaffles crispy again. In just a few minutes, an air fryer will dehydrate them and crisp them up nicely.

You can cook the chaffles 1-2 minutes per side in a dry pan, or you can position them in a 300-degree Fahrenheit oven for 3-4 minutes or until they are cooked clean. They probably won't get crispy, though, because they are going to retain too much humidity. If you don't have an air fryer, making smaller batches of chaffles and enjoying them fresh is your best bet. This means they're going to be tastier.

Chapter 5. Effective Tricks To Make A Great Chaffle

Gluten-free chaffles, combine two of America's most popular food items - cheese and waffles - and appear everywhere on social media. They are the undisputed stars of many Pinterest forums and stories on Instagram, and I have also found several groups of recipes on Facebook with tens of thousands of members. Join one of them, and you'll be bombarded with an endless stream of wonderful photos - and yes, most of them look really delicious. Although this concept is new for some of you, this overwhelming fashion seems to have emerged across America. It occurs mainly in eaters who follow a limited diet. Really, who can blame them: lovers of the ketogenic diet like to replace a low-carbohydrate bread that is cheap and easy to make, completely free of cereals. It is a fabulous solution for anyone who cannot eat gluten.

Ready to jump at the bar? Basic Chaffles only require a few daily ingredients: eggs and a handful of grated cheese with a little baking soda, if desired, to make it very light. Then you are only limited by your imagination and personal taste.

I personally prefer recipes for chaffles that contain coconut or almond flour for a less moist taste (you can only use protein to get the same effect). Extraordinary breads are even less spicy, use mayonnaise as a binder, and really taste like soft white bread and like a pillow. Sweet spots are seasoned with cream cheese. Optional additions give special notes - for example, cocoa powder, vanilla, chocolate chips, and/or cinnamon as a dessert of turkey or meat slices, jalapeno slices, herbal spices, or more seasoned garlic spices.

You can double the recipe below to make super tasty waffles (waffles are waffles, right?). But when you use it for sandwiches, the size of a mini waffle maker is perfect. Here are some tips for making perfect recipes:

- Preheat the waffle iron for a few minutes before using it and bring it to temperature.
- Even if your waffle iron is brand new and has a whole Teflon coating, spray the iron lightly with cooking spray or melt melted butter in all angles before adding the dough. If not, the stones can jam.
- Fill the hot iron with a light hand. The dough will come off after you close the lid, and if you mix it with the waffles, the dough will come out, leaving a terrible mess.
- Be patient. Resist the urge to open the waffle iron while still steaming.
- If you are serving more than one serving, keep the grill warm and crispy in the oven at 200 degrees.
- Don't be afraid to be creative. Try different types of cheese, herbs, food supplements, and side dishes.
- Don't check the dirt by opening the waffle iron too fast! You want it to cook until it's ripe and crispy. If nothing else, make the cooking side a little longer than you think.
- You can certainly experiment with other cheeses that are good for keto - goat cheese and halloumi work well - but mozzarella is usually recommended because it's mild and not as high as other choices.
- If you want more protein and flavor, you can also add 1 slice of ham when you mix eggs and cheese. Bacon can also work (enough if you follow a strict keto diet.)
- If you prefer sweet cubes, substitute mozzarella cream cheese. I like this tip! I can't imagine mozzarella on my cakes.
- Sprinkle a little extra cheese on waffle iron before adding the egg and cheese mixture to get a warm, crispy crust. My husband and I love this shrimp and cheese trick.
- It might be difficult to make it super crispy on the plate because the steam from the stew softens them like all waves. They are best eaten or frozen immediately, although I have found that a little almond flour helps the texture.
- Make loot: The mini-wafer maker in the dashboard is available in many good colors at prices under $ 15! You really can't go wrong with a waffle maker. If you don't already have a lot of keto bloggers, you're obsessed with Dash Mini Waffle Maker for Rifles. It is not only inexpensive but also multi-functional and available in many pleasant colors. Plus, it works really well; My best friend has been using it for years to make eggs for her children and swear by it. I personally use my Cuisinart classic waffle maker smoothly - it's only a few dollars more.
- Do more than you need - stains can be stored in the refrigerator for several days. I'm hot using my toaster, but you can also heat it in a pan on your stove.

- There are different variations! After reducing the basics, try some alternative recipes for a nasty touch on your own favorite recipe blog or magazine.

Learn from my mistakes...and successes. These tips should help.

Chapter 6. Pros and Cons Of Low Carb Diet

The carbohydrate-free diet has always been the most sought after and followed because it is considered quick and effective. But, what is a diet without carbohydrates? Before describing the benefits of a carbohydrate-free diet, it is imperative to clarify the "world" of low-carbohydrate diets.

It is not enough to eliminate bread, pasta, and pizza, from your diet in order to talk about a diet without carbohydrates. In fact, the term "carbohydrate-free diet" refers to a set of different dietary models (such as the best-known zone diet, Atkins diet, Dukan diet, Scarsdale diet, and ketogenic diet) which, while sharing a restriction of carbohydrates, have different metabolic patterns.

The carbohydrate-free diet that can be used in the Low Carb Diet, or the more extreme in No Carb Diet, has always been the most sought after and followed since it is considered quick and effective especially in the summer months, in which the race to lose weight in a short time it is more and more frequent. At this point, it is necessary to understand what a carbohydrate-free diet specifically consists of.

It is not enough to eliminate bread, pasta, and pizza from your diet, in order to talk about a diet without carbohydrates. In fact, the term diet without carbohydrates refers to a set of different dietary models, which, while sharing a restriction of carbohydrates, present different metabolic frameworks.

In fact, there are:

- Low Carb Diets, as diets containing less than 100 g of carbohydrates per day
- Very Low Carb Diet (very low carbohydrate content) as diets containing between 20 and 70 g of daily carbohydrates.
- Ketogenic diets, as diets with less than 20 g of carbohydrates per day.

While the former is medically safe, the other two should only be done under the supervision of a nutritionist. Declining the choice of a diet towards the one without carbohydrates mainly depends on the desire to want to lose weight, several scientific studies have shown that a low carbohydrate diet (obviously without excess) could improve health.

However, it is very important to know that too prolonged use of a low carbohydrate diet makes these initial advantages disappear, rather causing imbalances and disorders such as migraine, tiredness, difficulty concentrating and constipation, due to the low intake of carbohydrates.

What are the benefits of a carbohydrate-free diet, and how many pounds are lost?

The innate vocation of a diet without carbohydrates is certainly the slimming one, despite the fact that several scientific studies have also highlighted its interesting clinical properties. More precisely, a low-carbohydrate low-calorie diet, properly studied and well made, could:

- Improve the glycemic and lipidemic profile, also causing a lowering of blood glucose and cholesterol values;
- Strengthen the oxidative capacities, that is to say, enhance the metabolism, for short periods;
- Contribute to the rejuvenation of cellular structures;
- Accelerate weight loss.

And it is precisely this last point that pushes, especially in the summer, more and more people to adopt a dietary regime of this kind, and not without the right reasons. According to several studies, and therefore dispelling some myths, a restriction of carbohydrates, if carried out for a short period (max 3 weeks), could help support weight loss more intensely than other dietary regimens.

However, it would be advisable to know that in the medium and long term, this initial advantage linked to the restriction from carbohydrates would tend to decrease and then disappear. Therefore, the use of carbohydrate-free diets, for slimming purposes, could make sense as a "dietary start" and then absolutely switch to a Mediterranean diet.

Contraindications and side effects

Unfortunately, not all that glitters are gold. So, the very interesting metabolic and slimming properties of a well-structured carbohydrate-free diet often collide with the appearance of unpleasant side effects. Migraine, tiredness, and difficulty concentrating are the first side effects reported during the phases of strong restriction from carbohydrates, which often tend to regress spontaneously in the following days, to reappear more intense after several weeks.

Constipation and, more generally, disorders of the alve, tend to accompany the entire dietary period, especially if not adequately supported by a lot of water and probiotic supplements, useful for preserving the health of the intestine. However effective, and if supervised by a safe nutritionist, the carbohydrate-free diet, therefore, presents some inevitable contraindications for use.

Diabetic pathology, rather than other metabolic and psychiatric pathologies, particularly intense physical activity and advanced age, are just some of the conditions in which it would be preferable, even if only to lose weight, to resort to dietary schemes other than those without carbohydrates.

Sweets, biscuits, chips: difficult to do without. But how would our body change if we could limit its consumption? Foods rich in simple carbohydrates (that is, those that contain simple sugars or sugars added during storage and preparation), are rich in calories and do not bring nutrients to our diet. They don't make us feel fuller, on the contrary, they can also increase the sense of hunger. And, after an initial "hit of energy", they do not offer the right fuel to better enjoy the day.

Even though it is needed for our diet, excessive consumption may not be healthy. White rice, white pasta, white bread, desserts and sweets, artificial syrups, carbonated drinks, and candies: here are six things that happen when we decide to put them aside.

1. You will start burning fat. "Immediately eat this, not that!" the site says. "By reducing your consumption of carbohydrates, you will also decrease your personal daily amount of calories." In fact, when the body is forced not to draw on carbohydrates, it burns stored fat to produce energy. The site's advice is to do some exercise in the morning before breakfast. In this way, the body will burn all deposited fats instead of those contained in the food.

2. You will feel less hungry. It's not the calories that satiate your hunger, but the nutrients, like protein, fiber, or healthy fats. These components are absent in refined carbohydrates, which therefore end up filling our body only with useless calories. For this reason, after having made a feast, we can still feel hungry: the body, by taking carbohydrates, will always be looking for other food. By decreasing consumption, on the other hand, a sense of hunger will also decrease. "Eat this, not that!" is to start the day by eating something very protein and healthy like Greek yogurt or like eggs.

3. You will have a flatter belly. It is one of the most striking changes: when carbohydrates are replaced by foods rich in fiber, the belly may seem flatter. This is because the fibers, of which every diet should be rich, help to deflate belly fat. Many

sugars instead ferment in the intestine, making us feel swollen and making the belly appear larger than it really is. "Eat this, not that!" is to start replacing some unhealthy foods with healthier ones, and to eat nuts, sources of fiber and allies indigestion.

4. It will decrease the risk of suffering from illnesses such as diabetes. Simple sugars can be harmful to health in the long run. The more we digest, the more insulin our pancreas produces: this can lead to an increased risk of developing type 2 diabetes. The advice is to prefer complex carbohydrates, rich in fiber, more difficult for the body to digest: in this way, easy release of insulin will be prevented.

5. Your muscles will be stronger. According to the editors, taking only simple carbohydrates would not be good for muscle growth: "It is preferable to eat any other type of food, from meat to yogurt to ice cream - they write -. In part, this is it is due to the fact that carbohydrates lack proteins, which are real building blocks for muscle building and contribute to the health of the skin, hair, and nails ". Increasing the consumption of proteins and other nutrients can bring benefits to our body, without the need to take in additional calories. The site's advice is to prefer protein snacks over those of automatic machines.

6. You will feel more energetic. It is good to remember that carbohydrates must not be missing from a balanced diet: the body needs them to function properly, they are essential for brain health and for the functioning of the organs. Some, however, have a much more "fuel" effect than others: fruits, vegetables, bread, quinoa, and rice are just a few of these. They ensure those who eat energy for a long time and avoid some natural and typical changes caused by other simple carbohydrates.

Carbohydrate-free diet: the 10 useful recommendations

To optimize the results of a diet without carbohydrates, reduce side effects, and above all, to avoid recovering the lost pounds, it would be particularly useful not to forget these simple ten recommendations:

- o Make sure you are healthy;
- o Always keep active during the diet, avoiding particularly intense activities;
- o Avoid prolonging the diet without carbohydrates beyond 2 weeks, without the proper supervision of a nutritionist;
- o Remember to drink frequently, reaching at least 2 liters of water daily;
- o Prefer the consumption of raw vegetables, rich in mineral salts, vitamins, and fiber;
- o Take a probiotic supplement, always under the advice of a professional doctor, to preserve intestinal health;
- o Avoid consuming alcohol while dieting;
- o Change the daily menu as much as possible;
- o Gradually reintroduce carbohydrates in later stages;
- o Consult the professional immediately if you feel unwell.

Chapter 7. Keto Chaffle History

From time to time, the phenomenon of food breaks open and unexpected worlds, burning social media like wildfires and sweeping out innocents like tsunamis. What is this natural force?

This is the case for chaffle. Waffles made entirely of cheese and eggs. Sprinkle the minced cheese directly on a hot waffle iron, add some of the beaten eggs, put the cheese on top, and leave it to the waffle maker. This chaffle, which was virtually unknown a few weeks ago, sparked YouTube, Facebook, Reddit, Instagram, and Pinterest. In the first two weeks of August, all of Google's key results during this period were posted. Search soared: chaffle mania blossomed so quickly that it was not difficult to pinpoint the originator of the term. The only genius of Chaffle is like a You Tuber named the cat "Keto" Dos. See all original chaffle videos. Dos is delighted with her creation. Although dozens (or hundreds?) Of keto waffle recipes are already scattered around the Internet, the success of chaffle runaway seems to depend on several key factors.

You can't blame these chefs for trying to make the most sophisticated low carb waffles, but the complexity of such recipes means that they are likely to be used only on special weekends. Made with only one bowl and two pantry staples, the chaffle is easy enough to spin on a whimsical and whimsical basis.

This emphasis is built in from the start. In the original video, Dos called him a bread substitute, claiming that "the possibilities are endless." Double smash burger.

You cannot miss an ingenious name. This is undoubtedly a contributing factor in the dizziness and abandonment of chaffle head being obsessed with the new obsession. Chaffle was born according to the meme.

Chaffle is young enough, and no definitive recipe has yet appeared. As you read this, the discussion about good recipes on social media will intensify. Should I mix cheese with eggs? Is cream cheese more effective than cheddar cheese? Does a little almond flour improve texture?

The mileage of the chaffle may vary, but one point of consensus lies in the equipment you choose. The Dash Mini Waffle Maker, for only $ 9.99 on Amazon, was recommended in Cat Doss's original video. Because chaffle fever is so serious, some people actually upload UPS videos and distribute Dash Mini Waffle Makers.

Of course, the low carb world is no stranger to this phenomenon. Breakthrough recipes such as the original Fat Head Pizza that drew attention and exploded in early 2017 have become a staple of ketone-producing Canon. Zoodle has been steadily rising since 2014 and is now widely sold in mainstream grocery stores. Cauliflower rice-there is an annual spike that seems to be due to a New Year's resolution-there was the first big moment in January 2017.

What Keto Diet Is

This is what is called ketosis. In the first 3 to 6 months, a ketogenic diet can help you lose more weight than some other diets. This may be because the transformation of fat into energy requires more calories than the transformation of carbohydrates into energy. A high-fat, high-protein diet may also please you better, so you're eating less, but that's not yet confirmed. Typically, the more common ones are not serious: constipation, moderate low blood sugar, or indigestion. Low-carb diets can result in kidney stones or high acid levels in your bloodstream (acidosis) much less often. Other side effects may include headache, weakness, and irritability; bad breath; and fatigue.

Keto Chaffle Benefits

Appetite Management

On a keto diet, the appetite is likely to gain new control. It's a very common experience for hunger feelings to decrease dramatically, and studies prove it. It also makes it easier to fast intermittently, something that can increase efforts to reverse type 2 diabetes and accelerate weight loss, beyond the effects of keto only. Plus, you might be able to do so. Most people feel just the need to feed on a keto diet twice a day (often skipping breakfast), and some just eat once a day. Not having to fight hunger symptoms could also potentially help with issues such as obesity or drug addiction. Eventually, feeling happy can be part of the solution. Food should avoid being an opponent and turn into your partner, or just food, whatever you like.

This makes perfect sense as keto decreases blood sugar levels, eliminates the need for medicine, and reduces the potential negative effects of high levels of insulin.30 In the best case, long-term blood glucose can be so much changed that it returns to normal without treatment. In this context, reversal means progressing or getting worse the opposite of the disease. Lifestyle changes, though, only work when you do it. If a person returns to the lifestyle that he or she had when diabetes type 2 emerged and advanced, it is possible that they will recover and improve again over time.

How to reverse type 2 diabetes 200 + success stories Low carb and diabetes reversal Improved health markers many studies show that low-carb diets improve several major risk factors for heart disease, including the cholesterol profile, which includes cholesterol and triglycerides of high-density lipoprotein (HDL).

Total and low-density lipoprotein (LDL) cholesterol levels are usually affected modestly. Improved blood sugar levels, insulin levels, and blood pressure are also typical.33 These commonly improved markers are linked to something called "metabolic syndrome," an insulin-resistant condition that low-carb diets effectively treat. My health markers after 10 years on a keto diet

Also, when in keto, the brain does not need dietary carbs; it is common for people to experience an increase in energy. On keto. It is fuelled by ketones 24-7, along with your liver synthesizing a smaller amount of glucose.

This can sometimes lead to better focus and concentration and brain fog resolution with improved mental clarity. Keto and IBS A calmer stomach

A keto diet can lead to a calmer stomach, less gas. Yet the fat stores contain enough energy to last for weeks. Beyond this effect, another potential benefit is the decrease in the amount of body fat that can be obtained on a keto diet.

How To Maximize Stamina On a Keto Diet

Keto diet and epilepsy: Epilepsy the Ketogenic diet is a proven and often effective epilepsy medical therapy used since the 1920s. It has historically been used mainly for infants, but it has also helped adults in recent years. Using a Ketogenic diet for epilepsy will allow some people to take less or none anti-epileptic medications while being potentially seizure-free. This can reduce side effects of drugs and increase mental performance as a result.

How To Live Healthy From Low Carb

A low-carb diet is poor in carbs, found mainly in sugar, pasta, and bread. Then, you eat foods that include plant proteins, fats, and vegetables. Studies show that low-carb diets lead to weight loss and improved markers of health. For decades, these diets have been widely used and are recommended by many physicians. Best of all, calories do not usually need to be counted or special products used. All you need to do is eat whole foods that make a diet that is complete, nutritious, and filling. A low-carb diet means you're eating less carbohydrates and more fat. A low-carb, high-fat diet (LCHF) or a keto diet can also be called.

They have been advised for decades that fat is detrimental to our health. In the meantime, low-fat "diet" products have flooded supermarket shelves, often full of sugar. This was probably a major misunderstanding, which coincided with the onset of the epidemic of obesity. Although this does not prove causation, it is clear that the low-fat campaign did not prevent an increase in obesity, and it may have led to it. Studies now show no reason to be afraid of natural fats. Instead, your friend is on a low-carb diet. Just minimize your sugar and starch intake, and you can eat all the fat you need to be satisfied with. If you avoid sugar and starch, your blood sugar tends to stabilize, and the fat-storing hormone levels drop in insulin. This helps increase the burning of fat and makes you feel satiated, naturally reducing the intake of food and promoting weight loss. Studies show that a low-carb diet can make weight loss simpler and, among other advantages, regulate blood sugar.

Who is not expected to have a strict low-carb diet?

Some people can safely initiate a low-carb diet.13 But you may need some planning or modification in these three situations: are you taking diabetes medication, such as insulin, for example? Learn more Do you take high blood pressure medication? Discover more Are you breastfeeding at the moment? Learn more If you're not in any of these groups and you don't have any other severe chronic conditions, you're good to go!

Why do I have to try low-carb diet?

The issue with carbohydrates is that we tend to consume more than is actually needed for our bodies. For this reason, carbohydrates not burned off as energy are converted into sugars and stored in the body as fat. This is why, after the initial burst of energy from a meal filled with carbohydrates, you can feel sluggish.

A low-carb diet does not require you to completely cut carbohydrates out of your life. Instead, it tells you to limit the number of carbohydrates you eat to what you currently burn from physical activity, and to remember where the carbs you consume come from

What am I allowed to eat?

The issue that many people have with living low-carb is that they feel they have limited food options, but it doesn't have to be that way. In addition to plenty of delicious vegetables, a healthy low carb diet will include meat, fish, and eggs. A low-carb diet doesn't have to get repetitive as nuts and berries, as well as some healthy fats, can be included. As a result, many people living on low-carb diets consider that their diets are much more complex, flexible, and fascinating than before a low-carb diet is implemented. For those who want to lose weight, a low carb diet may be worth an attempt and are willing to cut down on carbs to do so. A low-carb diet can be healthy, nutritious, and tasty if you choose lean proteins as well as some fruits and vegetables, and even some fats and whole grains to make it a diet that you can consume and enjoy.

How To Boost Metabolism From Low Carb

The basic low-calorie diets do not work well when it comes to permanent weight loss. While it is true that in order to lose weight, you need to be in a calorie deficit, simple calorie counting is not a useful strategy for sustained weight loss.

Your metabolism is caused by a lot of weight loss. In a nutshell, your appetite is how much energy you use all day long, and how well the body is using that energy.

You have a great deal of control over how your metabolism works. Improving your metabolism makes weight loss faster, and maintaining your metabolism is a good predictor of a long, healthy life.

What does metabolism mean?

Your metabolism is the collection of daily energy-creating processes your body uses. Your metabolism fuels all you do, so becoming friendly with it is worthwhile. Which includes finding out how your metabolism can be assisted and rendered as high as possible?

The three main roles of your metabolism are:

1.   Converting food into energy for your cells

2.   Converting food into building blocks for proteins and fats to maintain the tissues of your body.

3.   Eliminating waste from your body. It produces energy, breaks down and rebuilds cells and bone, and removes waste, making it impossible to accurately measure the actual daily metabolism.

Chapter 8. Prepare Your Chaffles with 50 Delicious Recipes

1. Chocolate Melt Chaffles

Preparation Time: 15 minutes

Cooking Time: 36 minutes

Servings: 4

Ingredients

For the chaffles:

2 eggs, beaten

¼ cup finely grated Gruyere cheese

2 tbsp heavy cream

1 tbsp coconut flour

2 tbsp cream cheese, softened

3 tbsp unsweetened cocoa powder

2 tsp vanilla extract

A pinch of salt

For the chocolate sauce:

1/3 cup + 1 tbsp heavy cream

1 ½ oz unsweetened baking chocolate, chopped

1 ½ tsp sugar-free maple syrup

1 ½ tsp vanilla extract

Directions:

For the chaffles:

Preheat the waffle iron.

In a medium bowl, mix all the ingredients for the chaffles.

Open the iron and add a quarter of the mixture. Close and cook until crispy, 7 minutes.

Transfer the chaffle to a plate and make 3 more with the remaining batter.

For the chocolate sauce:

Pour the heavy cream into saucepan and simmer over low heat, 3 minutes.

Turn the heat off and add the chocolate. Allow melting for a few minutes and stir until fully melted 5 minutes.

Mix in the maple syrup and vanilla extract.

Assemble the chaffles in layers with the chocolate sauce sandwiched between each layer.

Slice and serve immediately.

Nutrition:

Calories 172

Fats 13.57g

Carbs 6.65g

Net Carbs 3.65g

Protein 5.76g

2. Chaffles with Keto Ice Cream

Preparation Time: 10 minutes

Cooking Time: 14 minutes

Servings: 2

Ingredients:

1 egg, beaten

½ cup finely grated mozzarella cheese

¼ cup almond flour

2 tbsp Swerve confectioner's sugar

1/8 tsp xanthan gum

Low-carb ice cream (flavor of your choice) for serving

Directions:

Preheat the waffle iron.

In a medium bowl, mix all the ingredients except the ice cream.

Open the iron and add half of the mixture. Close and cook until crispy, 7 minutes.

Transfer the chaffle to a plate and make the second one with the remaining batter.

On each chaffle, add a scoop of low carb ice cream, fold into half-moons and enjoy.

Nutrition:

Calories 89

Fats 6.48g

Carbs 1.67g

Net Carbs 1.37g

Protein 5.91g

3. Strawberry Shortcake Chaffle Bowls

Preparation Time: 10 minutes

Cooking Time: 28 minutes

Servings: 4

Ingredients:

1 egg, beaten

½ cup finely grated mozzarella cheese

1 tbsp almond flour

¼ tsp baking powder

2 drops cake batter extract

1 cup cream cheese, softened

1 cup fresh strawberries, sliced

1 tbsp sugar-free maple syrup

Directions:

Preheat a waffle bowl maker and grease lightly with cooking spray.

Meanwhile, in a medium bowl, whisk all the ingredients except the cream cheese and strawberries. Open the iron, pour in half of the mixture, cover, and cook until crispy, 6 to 7 minutes.

Remove the chaffle bowl onto a plate and set aside.

Make a second chaffle bowl with the remaining batter.

To serve, divide the cream cheese into the chaffle bowls and top with the strawberries.

Drizzle the filling with the maple syrup and serve.

Nutrition:

Calories 235

Fats 20.62g

Carbs 5.9g

Net Carbs 5g

Protein 7.51g

4. Chaffles with Raspberry Syrup

Preparation Time: 10 minutes

Cooking Time: 38 minutes

Servings: 4

Ingredients:

For the chaffles:

1 egg, beaten

½ cup finely shredded cheddar cheese

1 tsp almond flour

1 tsp sour cream

For the raspberry syrup:

1 cup fresh raspberries

¼ cup swerve sugar

¼ cup water

1 tsp vanilla extract

Directions:

For the chaffles:

Preheat the waffle iron.

Meanwhile, in a medium bowl, mix the egg, cheddar cheese, almond flour, and sour cream.

Open the iron, pour in half of the mixture, cover, and cook until crispy, 7 minutes.

Remove the chaffle onto a plate and make another with the remaining batter.

For the raspberry syrup:

Meanwhile, add the raspberries, swerve sugar, water, and vanilla extract to a medium pot. Set over low heat and cook until the raspberries soften and sugar becomes syrupy. Occasionally stir while mashing the raspberries as you go. Turn the heat off when your desired consistency is achieved and set aside to cool.

Drizzle some syrup on the chaffles and enjoy when ready.

Nutrition:

Calories 105

Fats 7.11g

Carbs 4.31g

Net Carbs 2.21g

Protein 5.83g

5. Chaffle Cannoli

Preparation Time: 15 minutes

Cooking Time: 28 minutes

Servings: 4

Ingredients:

For the chaffles:

1 large egg

1 egg yolk

3 tbsp butter, melted

1 tbsp swerve confectioner's

1 cup finely grated Parmesan cheese

2 tbsp finely grated mozzarella cheese

For the cannoli filling:

½ cup ricotta cheese

2 tbsp Swerve confectioner's sugar

1 tsp vanilla extract

2 tbsp unsweetened chocolate chips for garnishing

Directions:

Preheat the waffle iron.

Meanwhile, in a medium bowl, mix all the ingredients for the chaffles.

Open the iron, pour in a quarter of the mixture, cover, and cook until crispy, 7 minutes.

Remove the chaffle onto a plate and make 3 more with the remaining batter.

Meanwhile, for the cannoli filling:

Beat the ricotta cheese and swerve confectioner's sugar until smooth. Mix in the vanilla.

On each chaffle, spread some of the filling and wrap over.

Garnish the creamy ends with some chocolate chips.

Serve immediately.

Nutrition:

Calories 308

Fats 25.05g

Carbs 5.17g

Net Carbs 5.17g

Protein 15.18g

6. Blueberry Chaffles

Preparation Time: 10 minutes

Cooking Time: 28 minutes

Servings: 4

Ingredients:

1 egg, beaten

½ cup finely grated mozzarella cheese

1 tbsp cream cheese, softened

1 tbsp sugar-free maple syrup + extra for topping

½ cup blueberries

¼ tsp vanilla extract

Directions:

Preheat the waffle iron.

In a medium bowl, mix all the ingredients.

Open the iron, lightly grease with cooking spray and pour in a quarter of the mixture.

Close the iron and cook until golden brown and crispy, 7 minutes.

Remove the chaffle onto a plate and set aside.

Make the remaining chaffles with the remaining mixture.

Drizzle the chaffles with maple syrup and serve afterward.

Nutrition:

Calories 137

Fats 9.07g

Carbs 4.02g

Net Carbs 3.42g

Protein 9.59g

7. Nutter Butter Chaffles

Preparation Time: 15 minutes

Cooking Time: 14 minutes

Servings: 2

Ingredients:

For the chaffles:

2 tbsp sugar-free peanut butter powder

2 tbsp maple (sugar-free) syrup

1 egg, beaten

¼ cup finely grated mozzarella cheese

¼ tsp baking powder

¼ tsp almond butter

¼ tsp peanut butter extract

1 tbsp softened cream cheese

For the frosting:

½ cup almond flour

1 cup peanut butter

3 tbsp almond milk

½ tsp vanilla extract

½ cup maple (sugar-free) syrup

Directions:

Preheat the waffle iron.

Meanwhile, in a medium bowl, mix all the ingredients until smooth.

Open the iron and pour in half of the mixture.

Close the iron and cook until crispy, 6 to 7 minutes.

Remove the chaffle onto a plate and set aside.

Make a second chaffle with the remaining batter.

While the chaffles cool, make the frosting.

Pour the almond flour in a medium saucepan and stir-fry over medium heat until golden.

Transfer the almond flour to a blender and top with the remaining frosting ingredients. Process until smooth.

Spread the frosting on the chaffles and serve afterward.

Nutrition:

Calories 239

Fats 15.48g, Carbs 17.42g, Net Carbs 15.92g, Protein 7.52g

8. Chaffled Brownie Sundae

Preparation Time: 12 minutes

Cooking Time: 30 minutes

Servings: 4

Ingredients:

For the chaffles:

2 eggs, beaten

1 tbsp unsweetened cocoa powder

1 tbsp erythritol

1 cup finely grated mozzarella cheese

For the topping:

3 tbsp unsweetened chocolate, chopped

3 tbsp unsalted butter

½ cup swerve sugar

Low-carb ice cream for topping

1 cup whipped cream for topping

3 tbsp sugar-free caramel sauce

Directions:

For the chaffles:
Preheat the waffle iron.

Meanwhile, in a medium bowl, mix all the ingredients for the chaffles.

Open the iron, pour in a quarter of the mixture, cover, and cook until crispy, 7 minutes.

Remove the chaffle onto a plate and make 3 more with the remaining batter.

Plate and set aside.

For the topping:
Meanwhile, melt the chocolate and butter in a medium saucepan with occasional stirring, 2 minutes.

To Servings:

Divide the chaffles into wedges and top with the ice cream, whipped cream, and swirl the chocolate sauce and caramel sauce on top.

Serve immediately.

Nutrition:

Calories 165

Fats 11.39g, Carbs 3.81g, Net Carbs 2.91g, Protein 12.79g

9. Brie and Blackberry Chaffles

Preparation Time: 15 minutes

Cooking Time: 36 minutes

Servings: 4

Ingredients:

For the chaffles:

2 eggs, beaten

1 cup finely grated mozzarella cheese

For the topping:

1 ½ cups blackberries

1 lemon, 1 tsp zest and 2 tbsp juice

1 tbsp erythritol

4 slices Brie cheese

Directions:

For the chaffles:

Preheat the waffle iron.

Meanwhile, in a medium bowl, mix the eggs and mozzarella cheese.

Open the iron, pour in a quarter of the mixture, cover, and cook until crispy, 7 minutes.

Remove the chaffle onto a plate and make 3 more with the remaining batter.

Plate and set aside.

For the topping:

Preheat the oven to 350 F and line a baking sheet with parchment paper.

In a medium pot, add the blackberries, lemon zest, lemon juice, and erythritol. Cook until the blackberries break and the sauce thickens, 5 minutes. Turn the heat off.

Arrange the chaffles on the baking sheet and place two Brie cheese slices on each. Top with blackberry mixture and transfer the baking sheet to the oven.

Bake until the cheese melts, 2 to 3 minutes.

Remove from the oven, allow cooling and serve afterward.

Nutrition:

Calories 576

Fats 42.22g

Carbs 7.07g

Net Carbs 3.67g

Protein 42.35g

10.   Carrot Chaffle Cake

Preparation Time: 15 minutes

Cooking Time: 24 minutes

Servings: 6

Ingredients:

1 egg, beaten

2 tablespoons melted butter

½ cup carrot, shredded

¾ cup almond flour

1 teaspoon baking powder

2 tablespoons heavy whipping cream

2 tablespoons sweetener

1 tablespoon walnuts, chopped

1 teaspoon pumpkin spice

2 teaspoons cinnamon

Directions:

Preheat your waffle maker.

In a large bowl, combine all the ingredients.

Pour some of the mixture into the waffle maker.

Close and cook for 4 minutes.

Repeat steps until all the remaining batter has been used.

Nutrition:

Calories 294

Total Fat 26.7g

Saturated Fat 12g

Cholesterol 133mg

Sodium 144mg

Potassium 421mg

Total Carbohydrate 11.6g

Dietary Fiber 4.5g

Protein 6.8g

Total Sugars 1.7g

11.   Cereal Chaffle Cake

Preparation Time: 5 minutes

Cooking Time: 8 minutes

Servings: 2

Ingredients:

1 egg

2 tablespoons almond flour

½ teaspoon coconut flour

1 tablespoon melted butter

1 tablespoon cream cheese

1 tablespoon plain cereal, crushed

¼ teaspoon vanilla extract

¼ teaspoon baking powder

1 tablespoon sweetener

1/8 teaspoon xanthan gum

Directions:

Plug in your waffle maker to preheat.

Add all the ingredients in a large bowl.

Mix until well blended.

Let the batter rest for 2 minutes before cooking.

Pour half of the mixture into the waffle maker. Seal and cook for 4 minutes.

Make the next chaffle using the same steps.

Nutrition:

Calories154

Total Fat 21.2g

Saturated Fat 10 g

Cholesterol 113.3mg

Sodium 96.9mg

Potassium 453 mg

Total Carbohydrate 5.9g

Dietary Fiber 1.7g

Protein 4.6g

Total Sugars 2.7g

12.   Ham, Cheese & Tomato Chaffle Sandwich

Preparation Time: 5 minutes

Cooking Time: 10 minutes

Servings: 2

Ingredients:

1 teaspoon olive oil

2 slices ham

4 basic chaffles

1 tablespoon mayonnaise

2 slices Provolone cheese

1 tomato, sliced

Directions:

Add the olive oil to a pan over medium heat.

Cook the ham for 1 minute per side.

Spread the chaffles with mayonnaise.

Top with the ham, cheese and tomatoes.

Top with another chaffle to make a sandwich.

Nutrition:

Calories 198

Total Fat 14.7g

Saturated Fat 6.3g

Cholesterol 37mg

Sodium 664mg

Total Carbohydrate 4.6g

Dietary Fiber 0.7g

Total Sugars 1.5g

Protein 12.2g

Potassium 193mg

13.   Broccoli & Cheese Chaffle

Preparation Time: 5 minutes

Cooking Time: 8 minutes

Servings: 2

Ingredients:

¼ cup broccoli florets

1 egg, beaten

1 tablespoon almond flour

¼ teaspoon garlic powder

½ cup cheddar cheese

Directions:

Preheat your waffle maker.

Add the broccoli to the food processor.

Pulse until chopped.

Add to a bowl.

Stir in the egg and the rest of the ingredients.

Mix well.

Pour half of the batter to the waffle maker.

Cover and cook for 4 minutes.

Repeat procedure to make the next chaffle.

Nutrition:

Calories 170

Total Fat 13 g

Saturated Fat 7 g

Cholesterol 112 mg

Sodium 211 mg

Potassium 94 mg

Total Carbohydrate 2 g

Dietary Fiber 1 g

Protein 11 g

Total Sugars 1 g

14.   Chaffle with Sausage Gravy

Preparation Time: 5 minutes

Cooking Time: 15 minutes

Servings: 2

Ingredients:

¼ cup sausage, cooked

3 tablespoons chicken broth

2 teaspoons cream cheese

2 tablespoons heavy whipping cream

¼ teaspoon garlic powder

Pepper to taste

2 basic chaffles

Directions:

Add the sausage, broth, cream cheese, cream, garlic powder and pepper to a pan over medium heat.

Bring to a boil and then reduce heat.

Simmer for 10 minutes or until the sauce has thickened.

Pour the gravy on top of the basic chaffles

Serve.

Nutrition:

Calories 212

Total Fat 17 g

Saturated Fat 10 g

Cholesterol 134 mg

Sodium 350 mg

Potassium 133 mg

Total Carbohydrate 3 g

Dietary Fiber 1 g

Protein 11 g

Total Sugars 1 g

15.   Barbecue Chaffle

Preparation Time: 5 minutes

Cooking Time: 8 minutes

Servings: 2

Ingredients:

1 egg, beaten

½ cup cheddar cheese, shredded

½ teaspoon barbecue sauce

¼ teaspoon baking powder

Directions:

Plug in your waffle maker to preheat.

Mix all the ingredients in a bowl.

Pour half of the mixture to your waffle maker.

Cover and cook for 4 minutes.

Repeat the same steps for the next barbecue chaffle.

Nutrition:

Calories 295

Total Fat 23 g

Saturated Fat 13 g

Cholesterol 223 mg

Sodium 414 mg

Potassium 179 mg

Total Carbohydrate 2 g

Dietary Fiber 1 g

Protein 20 g

Total Sugars 1 g

16.   Bacon Chaffle Omelette

Preparation time: 5 min

Cooking time: 10 min

Servings: 2

Ingredients:

2 slices bacon, raw

1 egg

1 tsp maple extract, optional

1 tsp all spices

Directions:

Put the bacon slices in a blender and turn it on.

Once ground up, add in the egg and all spices. Go on blending until liquefied.

Heat your waffle maker on the highest setting and spray with non-stick cooking spray.

Pour half the omelet into the waffle maker and cook for 5 minutes max.

Remove the crispy omelet and repeat the same steps with rest batter.

Enjoy warm.

Nutrition:

Calories per Serving: 59 Kcal

Fats: 4.4 g

Carbs: 1 g

Protein: 5 g

17.   Bacon & Chicken Ranch Chaffle

Preparation Time: 5 minutes

Cooking Time: 8 minutes

Servings: 2

Ingredients:

1 egg

¼ cup chicken cubes, cooked

1 slice bacon, cooked and chopped

¼ cup cheddar cheese, shredded

1 teaspoon ranch dressing powder

Directions:

Preheat your waffle maker.

In a bowl, mix all the ingredients.

Add half of the mixture to your waffle maker.

Cover and cook for 4 minutes.

Make the second chaffle using the same steps.

Nutrition:

Calories 200

Total Fat 14 g

Saturated Fat 6 g

Cholesterol 129 mg

Total Carbohydrate 2 g

Dietary Fiber 1 g

Protein 16 g

Total Sugars 1 g

18.   Pumpkin & Pecan Chaffle

Preparation Time: 5 minutes

Cooking Time: 10 minutes

Servings: 2

Ingredients:

1 egg, beaten

½ cup mozzarella cheese, grated

½ teaspoon pumpkin spice

1 tablespoon pureed pumpkin

2 tablespoons almond flour

1 teaspoon sweetener

2 tablespoons pecans, chopped

Directions:

Turn on the waffle maker.

Beat the egg in a bowl.

Stir in the rest of the ingredients.

Pour half of the mixture into the device.

Seal the lid.

Cook for 5 minutes.

Remove the chaffle carefully.

Repeat the steps to make the second chaffle.

Nutrition:

Calories 210

Total Fat 17 g

Saturated Fat 10 g

Cholesterol 110 mg

Sodium 250 mg

Potassium 570 mg

Total Carbohydrate 4.6 g

Dietary Fiber 1.7 g

Protein 11 g

Total Sugars 2 g

19.   Cheeseburger Chaffle

Preparation Time: 15 minutes

Cooking Time: 15 minutes

Servings: 2

Ingredients:

1 lb. ground beef

1 onion, minced

1 tsp. parsley, chopped

1 egg, beaten

Salt and pepper to taste

1 tablespoon olive oil

4 basic chaffles

2 lettuce leaves

2 cheese slices

1 tablespoon dill pickles

Ketchup

Mayonnaise

Directions:

In a large bowl, combine the ground beef, onion, parsley, egg, salt and pepper.

Mix well.

Form 2 thick patties.

Add olive oil to the pan.

Place the pan over medium heat.

Cook the patty for 3 to 5 minutes per side or until fully cooked.

Place the patty on top of each chaffle.

Top with lettuce, cheese and pickles.

Squirt ketchup and mayo over the patty and veggies.

Top with another chaffle.

Nutrition:

Calories 325

Total Fat 16.3g

Saturated Fat 6.5g

Cholesterol 157mg

Sodium 208mg

Total Carbohydrate 3g

Dietary Fiber 0.7g

Total Sugars 1.4g

Protein 39.6g

Potassium 532mg

## 20.	Double Choco Chaffle

Preparation Time: 5 minutes

Cooking Time: 10 minutes

Servings: 2

Ingredients:

1 egg

2 teaspoons coconut flour

2 tablespoons sweetener

1 tablespoon cocoa powder

¼ teaspoon baking powder

1 oz. cream cheese

½ teaspoon vanilla

1 tablespoon sugar-free chocolate chips

Directions:

Put all the ingredients in a large bowl.

Mix well.

Pour half of the mixture into the waffle maker.

Seal the device.

Cook for 4 minutes.

Uncover and transfer to a plate to cool.

Repeat the procedure to make the second chaffle.

Nutrition:

Calories 171

Total Fat 10.7g

Saturated Fat 5.3g

Cholesterol 97mg

Sodium 106mg

Potassium 179mg

Total Carbohydrate 3g

Dietary Fiber 4.8g

Protein 5.8g

Total Sugars 0.4g

21.   Cream Cheese Chaffle

Preparation Time: 5 minutes

Cooking Time: 8 minutes

Servings: 2

Ingredients:

1 egg, beaten

1 oz. cream cheese

½ teaspoon vanilla

4 teaspoons sweetener

¼ teaspoon baking powder

Cream cheese

Directions:

Preheat your waffle maker.

Add all the ingredients in a bowl.

Mix well.

Pour half of the batter into the waffle maker.

Seal the device.

Cook for 4 minutes.

Remove the chaffle from the waffle maker.

Make the second one using the same steps.

Spread remaining cream cheese on top before serving.

Nutrition:

Calories 169

Total Fat 14.3g

Saturated Fat 7.6g

Cholesterol 195mg

Sodium 147mg

Potassium 222mg

Total Carbohydrate 4g

Dietary Fiber 4g

Protein 7.7g

Total Sugars 0.7g

22.   Scrambled Egg Stuffed Chaffles

Preparation Time: 15 minutes

Cooking Time: 28 minutes

Servings: 4

Ingredients:

For the chaffles:

1 cup finely grated cheddar cheese

2 eggs, beaten

For the egg stuffing:

1 tbsp olive oil

4 large eggs

1 small green bell pepper, deseeded and chopped

1 small red bell pepper, deseeded and chopped

Salt and freshly ground black pepper to taste

2 tbsp grated Parmesan cheese

Directions:

For the chaffles:

Preheat the waffle iron.

In a medium bowl, mix the cheddar cheese and egg.

Open the iron, pour in a quarter of the mixture, close, and cook until crispy, 6 to 7 minutes.

Plate and make three more chaffles using the remaining mixture.

For the egg stuffing:
Meanwhile, heat the olive oil in a medium skillet over medium heat on a stovetop.

In a medium bowl, beat the eggs with the bell peppers, salt, black pepper, and Parmesan cheese.

Pour the mixture into the skillet and scramble until set to your likeness, 2 minutes.

Between two chaffles, spoon half of the scrambled eggs and repeat with the second set of chaffles.

Serve afterward.

Nutrition:

Calories 387

Fats 22.52g

Carbs 18.12g

Net Carbs 17.52g

Protein 27.76g

23.   Basic Keto Chaffle Recipe

Preparation Time: 5 mins

Cooking Time: 8 mins

Servings: 1

Ingredients:

1 egg

1/2 cup cheddar cheese, shredded

Directions:

Turn waffle maker on or plug it in so that it heats and grease both sides.

In a small bowl, crack an egg, then add the 1/2 cup cheddar cheese and stir to combine.

Pour 1/2 of the batter in the waffle maker and close the top.

Cook for 3-4 minutes or until it reaches desired doneness.

Carefully remove from waffle maker and set aside for 2-3 minutes to give it time to crisp.

Follow the instructions again to make the second chaffle.

Nutrition:

Calories: 291kcal

Carbohydrates: 1g

Protein: 20g

Fat: 23g

Saturated Fat: 13g

Cholesterol: 223mg

Sodium: 413mg

Potassium: 116mg

Sugar: 1g

Vitamin A: 804IU

Calcium: 432mg

Iron: 1mg

Variations to the Basic Keto Chaffle Recipe:

Experiment with different kinds of cheese such as Monterrey Jack, Colby, mozzarella cheese, etc. You could even combine two different kinds of cheese for added flavor.

Add spices such as garlic powder, Italian seasoning, Everything But the Bagel seasoning, or red pepper flakes to turn it up a notch

Add a tsp of coconut flour or a tablespoon of almond flour along with 1/4 tsp baking powder and a pinch of salt.

Thinly chopped peppers, onions, or jalapenos can add flavor and texture.

Keep it sugar-free by adding keto-friendly sweeteners like Lakanto Monkfruit or Swerve to make a sweet Chaffle.

24.   Chocolate Chip Chaffle Keto Recipe

Preparation Time: 5 mins

Cooking Time: 8 mins

Serving: 1

Ingredients:

1 egg

1 tbsp heavy whipping cream

1/2 tsp coconut flour

1 3/4 tsp Lakanto monk fruit golden can use more or less to adjust sweetness

1/4 tsp baking powder

pinch of salt

1 tbsp Lily's Chocolate Chips

Directions:

Turn on the waffle maker so that it heats up.

In a small bowl, combine all ingredients except the chocolate chips and stir well until combined.

Grease waffle maker, then pour half of the batter onto the bottom plate of the waffle maker. Sprinkle a few chocolate chips on top and then close.

Cook for 3-4 minutes or until the chocolate chip chaffle dessert is golden brown, then remove from waffle maker with a fork, being careful not to burn your fingers.

Repeat with the rest of the batter.

Let chaffle sit for a few minutes so that it begins to crisp. If desired, serve with sugar-free whipped topping.

Nutrition:

Calories: 146kcal

Carbohydrates: 7g

Protein: 6g

Fat: 10g

Saturated Fat: 7g

Fiber: 3g

Sugar: 1g

25.   Keto Blueberry Chaffle

Preparation Time: 3 minutes

Cooking Time: 15 minutes

Servings: 5

Ingredients:

1 cup of mozzarella cheese

2 tablespoons almond flour

1 tsp baking powder

2 eggs

1 tsp cinnamon

2 tsp of Swerve

3 tablespoon blueberries

Directions:

Heat up your Dash mini waffle maker.

In a mixing bowl, add the mozzarella cheese, almond flour, baking powder, eggs, cinnamon, swerve, and blueberries. Mix well, so all the ingredients are mixed together.

Spray your mini waffle maker with nonstick cooking spray.

Add in a little bit less than 1/4 a cup of blueberry keto waffle batter.

Close the lid and cook the chaffle for 3-5 minutes. Check it at the 3-minute mark to see if it is crispy and brown. If it is not or it sticks to the top of the waffle machine, close the lid and cook for 1-2 minutes longer.

Serve with a sprinkle of swerve confectioners sugar or keto syrup.

Nutrition:

Calories: 116kcal

Carbohydrates: 3g

Protein: 8g

Fat: 8g

Saturated Fat: 4g

Cholesterol: 83mg

Sodium: 166mg

Potassium: 142mg

Fiber: 1g

Sugar: 1g

Vitamin A: 246IU

Vitamin C: 1mg

Calcium: 177mg, Iron: 1mg

26.   Cinnamon Roll Keto Chaffles

Preparation Time: 5 minutes

Cooking Time: 10 minutes

Servings: 3

Ingredients:

Cinnamon Roll Chaffle Ingredients:

1/2 cup mozzarella cheese

1 tablespoon almond flour

1/4 tsp baking powder

1 egg

1 tsp cinnamon

1 tsp Granulated Swerve

Cinnamon roll swirl Ingredients:

1 tbsp butter

1 tsp cinnamon

2 tsp confectioners swerve

Keto Cinnamon Roll Glaze

1 tablespoon butter

1 tablespoon cream cheese

1/4 tsp vanilla extract

2 tsp swerve confectioners

Directions:

Plug in your Mini Dash Waffle maker and let it heat up.

In a small bowl mix the mozzarella cheese, almond flour, baking powder, egg, 1 teaspoon cinnamon, and 1 teaspoon swerve granulated and set aside.

In another small bowl, add a tablespoon of butter, 1 teaspoon cinnamon, and 2 teaspoons of swerve confectioners sweetener.

Microwave for 15 seconds and mix well.

Spray the waffle maker with nonstick spray and add 1/3 of the batter to your waffle maker. Swirl in 1/3 of the cinnamon, swerve, and butter mixture onto the top of it. Close the waffle maker and let cook for 3-4 minutes.

When the first cinnamon roll chaffle is done, make the second and then make the third.

While the third chaffle is cooking place 1 tablespoon butter and 1 tablespoon of cream cheese in a small bowl. Heat in the microwave for 10-15 seconds. Start at 10, and if the cream cheese is not soft enough to mix with the butter heat for an additional 5 seconds.

Add the vanilla extract, and the swerve confectioners sweetener to the butter and cream cheese and mix well using a whisk.

Drizzle keto cream cheese glaze on top of chaffle.

Nutrition:

Calories: 180kcal

Carbohydrates: 3g

Protein: 7g

Fat: 16g

Saturated Fat: 9g

Cholesterol: 95mg

Sodium: 221mg

Potassium: 77mg

Fiber: 1g

Sugar: 1g

Vitamin A: 505IU

Calcium: 148mg

Iron: 1mg

27.   Keto Chaffle Taco Shells

Preparation Time: 5 minutes

Cooking Time: 20 minutes

Servings: 5

Ingredients:

1 tablespoon almond flour

1 cup taco blend cheese

2 eggs

1/4 tsp taco seasoning

Directions:

In a bowl, mix almond flour, taco blend cheese, eggs, and taco seasoning. I find it easiest to mix everything using a fork.

Add 1.5 tablespoons of taco chaffle batter to the waffle maker at a time — Cook chaffle batter in the waffle maker for 4 minutes.

Remove the taco chaffle shell from the waffle maker and drape over the side of a bowl. I used my pie pan because it was what I had on hand, but just about any bowl will work.

Continue making chaffle taco shells until you are out of batter. Then fill your taco shells with taco meat, your favorite toppings, and enjoy!

Nutrition:

Calories: 113kcal

Carbohydrates: 1g

Protein: 8g

Fat: 9g

Saturated Fat: 4g

Cholesterol: 87mg

Sodium: 181mg

Potassium: 43mg

Fiber: 1g

Sugar: 1g

Vitamin A: 243IU

Calcium: 160mg

Iron: 1mg

28.   Garlic Bread Chaffles

Preparation Time: 3 minutes

Cooking Time: 11 minutes

Servings: 2

Ingredients:

1/2 cup shredded Mozzarella cheese

1 egg

1/2 tsp basil

1/4 tsp garlic powder

1 tbsp almond flour

1 tbsp butter

1/4 tsp garlic powder

1/4 cup shredded mozzarella cheese

Directions:

Heat up your Dash mini waffle maker.

In a small bowl, mix the egg, 1/2 tsp basil, 1/4 tsp garlic powder, 1 tablespoon almond flour and 1/2 cup Mozzarella Cheese. Add 1/2 of the batter into your mini waffle maker and cook for 4 minutes. If they are still a bit uncooked, leave it cooking for another 2 minutes. Then cook the rest of the batter to make a second chaffle.

In a small bowl, add 1 tablespoon butter and 1/4 tsp garlic powder and melt in the microwave. It will take about 25 seconds or so, depending on your microwave.

Place the chaffles on a baking sheet and use a rubber brush to spread the butter and garlic mixture on top.

Add 1/8th a cup of cheese on top of each chaffle.

Put chaffles in the oven or a toaster oven at 400 degrees and cook until the cheese is melted.

Nutrition:

Calories: 231kcal

Carbohydrates: 2g

Protein: 13g

Fat: 19g

Saturated Fat: 10g

Cholesterol: 130mg

Sodium: 346mg

Potassium: 52mg

Fiber: 1g

Sugar: 1g

29.   Peanut Butter Chaffle

Preparation Time: 3 minutes

Cooking Time: 8 minutes

Servings: 2

Ingredients:

1 egg

1/2 cup mozzarella cheese shredded

3 tablespoons swerve granulated

2 tbsp peanut butter

Directions:

Heat up your waffle maker.

In a bowl, mix the peanut butter, egg, granulated swerve, and mozzarella cheese.

Pour half of the chaffle batter into the waffle maker and cook for 4 minutes.

Carefully remove once cooked and place on a plate to cool. The chaffle will be a little flimsy when you remove it, but it will stiffen up as it cools.

Next, cook your second chaffle and let it sit for 2 minutes after you cook it.

Nutrition:

Calories: 210kcal

Carbohydrates: 4g

Protein: 13g

Fat: 16g

Saturated Fat: 6g

Cholesterol: 104mg

Sodium: 280mg

Potassium: 155mg

Fiber: 1g

Sugar: 2g

Vitamin A: 308IU

Calcium: 161mg

Iron: 1mg

30.   Pumpkin Chocolate Chip Chaffles

Preparation Time: 4 minutes

Cooking Time: 12 minutes

Servings: 3

Ingredients:

1/2 cup shredded mozzarella cheese

4 teaspoons pumpkin puree

1 egg

2 tablespoons granulated Swerve

1/4 tsp pumpkin pie spice

4 teaspoons sugar-free chocolate chips

1 tablespoon almond flour

Directions:

Plug in your waffle maker.

In a small bowl, mix the pumpkin puree and egg. Make sure you mix it well, so all the pumpkin is mixed with the egg.

Next, add in the mozzarella cheese, almond flour, swerve and add pumpkin spice and mix well.

Then add in your sugar-free chocolate chips

Add half the keto pumpkin pie Chaffle mix to the Dish Mini waffle maker at a time. Cook chaffle batter in the waffle maker for 4 minutes.

Do not open before the 4 minutes is up. It is very important that you do not open the waffle maker before the 4-minute mark. After that you can open it to check it and make sure it is cooked all the way, but with these chaffles keeping the lid closed the whole time is very important.

When the first one is completely done cooking cook the second one.

Enjoy with some swerve confectioners sweetener or whipped cream on top.

Nutrition:

Calories: 93kcal

Carbohydrates: 2g

Protein: 7g

Fat: 7g

Saturated Fat: 3g

Cholesterol: 69mg

Sodium: 138mg

Potassium: 48mg

Fiber: 1g

Sugar: 1g

Vitamin A: 1228IU

Calcium: 107mg

Iron: 1mg

31.   Broccoli & Cheese Chaffle

Preparation Time: 2 minutes

Cooking Time: 8 minutes

Servings: 2

Ingredients:

1/2 cup cheddar cheese

1/4 cup fresh chopped broccoli

1 egg

1/4 teaspoon garlic powder

1 tablespoon almond flour

Directions:

In a bowl, mix almond flour, cheddar cheese, egg, and garlic powder. I find it easiest to mix everything using a fork.

Add half the Broccoli and Cheese Chaffle batter to the Dish Mini waffle maker at a time.

Cook chaffle batter in the waffle maker for 4 minutes.

Let each chaffle sit for 1-2 minutes on a plate to firm up. Enjoy alone or dipping in sour cream or ranch dressing.

Nutrition:

Calories: 170kcal

Carbohydrates: 2g

Protein: 11g

Fat: 13g

Saturated Fat: 7g

Cholesterol: 112mg

Sodium: 211mg

Potassium: 94mg

Fiber: 1g

Sugar: 1g

Vitamin A: 473IU

Vitamin C: 10mg

Calcium: 229mg

Iron: 1mg

32.   Peanut Butter Chocolate Chip Chaffle

Preparation Time: 2 minutes

Cooking Time: 8 minutes

Servings: 2

Ingredients:

1 egg.

1/4 cup shredded mozzarella cheese

2 tablespoons creamy Peanut Butter.

1 tablespoon Almond Flour.

1 tablespoon Granulated Swerve.

1 teaspoon Vanilla extract.

1 tablespoon low carb chocolate chips.

Directions:

Plug in your waffle maker.

In a small bowl, mix the peanut butter and egg. Make sure you mix it well, so all the peanut butter is mixed with the egg.

Next, add in the mozzarella cheese, almond flour, swerve and chocolate chips and mix well.

Add half the keto peanut butter chocolate chip Chaffle mix to the Dish Mini waffle maker at a time. Cook chaffle batter in the waffle maker for 4 minutes.

When the first one is completely done cooking cook the second one.

Enjoy with some swerve confectioners sweetener or whipped cream on top.

Nutrition:

Calories: 193kcal

Carbohydrates: 5g

Protein: 11g

Fat: 15g

Saturated Fat: 4g

Cholesterol: 93mg

Sodium: 193mg

Potassium: 134mg

Fiber: 1g

Sugar: 2g

Vitamin A: 213IU

Calcium: 97mg

Iron: 1mg

33.   Broccoli & Cheese Chaffle

Preparation Time: 2 minutes

Cooking Time: 8 minutes

Servings: 2

Ingredients:

1/2 cup cheddar cheese

1/4 cup fresh chopped broccoli

1 egg

1/4 teaspoon garlic powder

1 tablespoon almond flour

Directions:

In a bowl, mix almond flour, cheddar cheese, egg, and garlic powder. I find it easiest to mix everything using a fork.

Add half the Broccoli and Cheese Chaffle batter to the Dish Mini waffle maker at a time.

Cook chaffle batter in the waffle maker for 4 minutes.

Let each chaffle sit for 1-2 minutes on a plate to firm up. Enjoy alone or dipping in sour cream or ranch dressing.

Nutrition:

Calories: 170kcal

Carbohydrates: 2g

Protein: 11g

Fat: 13g

Saturated Fat: 7g

Cholesterol: 112mg

Sodium: 211mg

Potassium: 94mg

Fiber: 1g

Sugar: 1g

Vitamin A: 473IU

Vitamin C: 10mg

Calcium: 229mg

Iron: 1mg

34.   French Dip Keto Chaffle Sandwich

Preparation Time: 5 mins

Cooking Time: 12 mins

Servings: 2

Ingredients:

1 egg white

1/4 cup mozzarella cheese, shredded (packed)

1/4 cup sharp cheddar cheese, shredded (packed)

3/4 tsp water

1 tsp coconut flour

1/4 tsp baking powder

Pinch of salt

Directions:

Preheat oven to 425 degrees. Plug the Dash Mini Waffle Maker in the wall and grease lightly once it is hot.

Combine all of the ingredients in a bowl and stir to combine.

Spoon out 1/2 of the batter on the waffle maker and close lid. Set a timer for 4 minutes and do not lift the lid until the cooking time is complete. Lifting beforehand can cause the Chaffle keto sandwich recipe to separate and stick to the waffle iron. You have to let it cook the entire 4 minutes before lifting the lid.

Remove the chaffle from the waffle iron and set aside. Repeat the same steps above with the rest of the chaffle batter.

Cover a cookie sheet with parchment paper and place chaffles a few inches apart.

Add 1/4 to 1/3 cup of the slow cooker keto roast beef from the following recipe. Make sure to drain the excess broth/gravy before adding to the top of the chaffle.

Add a slice of deli cheese or shredded cheese on top. Swiss and provolone are both great options.

Place on the top rack of the oven for 5 minutes so that the cheese can melt. If you'd like the cheese to bubble and begin to brown, turn oven to broil for 1 min. (The swiss cheese may not brown)

Enjoy open-faced with a small bowl of beef broth for dipping.

Note:
The nutritional information provided is only for the chaffles sandwich keto recipe. It does not include the beef or added cheese on top of the sandwich. That info will vary depending on the cut of beef you use and type of cheese.

Nutrition:

Calories: 118kcal

Carbohydrates: 2g, Protein: 9g, Fat: 8g

Fiber: 1g

35. Blackberry Chaffle

Preparation time: 5 minutes

Cooking time: 8 minutes

Servings: 4

Ingredients:

¼ cup cream cheese, soft

¼ cup blackberries

2 tablespoons almond flour

1 egg, whisked

1 tablespoon stevia

½ teaspoon baking soda

Directions:

In a bowl, mix the cream cheese with the berries and the other ingredients and whisk well. Heat up the waffle iron over high heat, pour ¼ of the batter, close the waffle maker, cook for 8 minutes and transfer to a plate.

Repeat with the rest of the batter and serve the chaffles warm.

Nutrition:

calories 160

fat 9.3, carbs 3.4, protein 3.5

36.   Coconut Chaffle

Preparation time: 5 minutes

Cooking time: 10 minutes

Servings: 4

Ingredients:

½ cup cream cheese, soft

1 tablespoon coconut flesh, unsweetened and shredded

2 teaspoons coconut oil, melted

1 tablespoon coconut flour

3 eggs, whisked

1 tablespoon erythritol

1 teaspoon vanilla extract

½ teaspoon almond extract

Directions:

In a bowl, combine the cream cheese with the melted coconut oil and the other ingredients and whisk well. Heat up the waffle iron over high heat, pour ¼ of the batter, close the waffle maker, cook for 10 minutes and transfer to a plate. Repeat with the rest of the batter and serve the chaffles warm.

Nutrition: calories 230, fat 11.2, fiber 1.2, carbs 3.4, protein 5.56

37.   Mint Chaffle

Preparation time: 5 minutes

Cooking time: 5 minutes

Servings: 2

Ingredients:

½ cup cream cheese, soft

1 tablespoon almond flour

½ tablespoon coconut flour

2 eggs whisked

1 tablespoon swerve

2 tablespoons mint, chopped

1 teaspoon vanilla extract

½ teaspoon almond extract

Directions:

In a bowl, combine the cream cheese with the flour and the other ingredients and whisk well.

Heat up the waffle iron over high heat, pour half of the batter, close the waffle maker, cook for 5 minutes and transfer to a plate.

Repeat with the other part of the batter and serve the chaffles warm.

Nutrition:

calories 182, fat 8.3, fiber 1.2, carbs 3.4, protein 6.5

38.　　Nuts Chaffle

Preparation time: 5 minutes

Cooking time: 8 minutes

Servings: 4

Ingredients:

2 tablespoons almonds, chopped

2 tablespoons walnuts, chopped

1 tablespoon stevia

½ cup cream cheese, soft

2 eggs, whisked

1 tablespoon almond flour

1 tablespoon coconut flour

½ teaspoon almond extract

Directions:

In a blender, mix the almonds with the walnuts, cream cheese and the other ingredients and pulse well.

Heat up the waffle iron over high heat, pour ¼ of the batter, close the waffle maker, cook for 5 minutes and transfer to a plate.

Repeat with the other part of the batter and serve.

Nutrition:

calories 200, fat 9.34, fiber 2.2, carbs 4.4, protein 8.4

39.   Rhubarb Chaffles

Preparation time: 5 minutes

Cooking time: 6 minutes

Servings: 3

Ingredients:

½ cup rhubarb, chopped

¼ cup heavy cream

3 tablespoons cream cheese, soft

2 tablespoons almond flour

2 eggs, whisked

2 tablespoons swerve

½ teaspoon vanilla extract

½ teaspoon nutmeg, ground

Directions:

In a bowl, mix the rhubarb with the cream, cream cheese and the other ingredients and whisk well.

Heat up the waffle iron over high heat, pour 1/3 of the batter, close the waffle maker, cook for 5 minutes and transfer to a plate.

Repeat with the rest of the chaffle batter and serve.

Nutrition:

calories 180, fat 4, fiber 1.2, carbs 2, protein 2.4

40.   Basil Cherry Tomato Chaffle

Preparation time: 5 minutes

Cooking time: 6 minutes

Servings: 2

Ingredients:

1 egg, whisked

½ cup mozzarella, shredded

1 cup cherry tomatoes, cubed

2 tablespoons basil, chopped

2 tablespoons cream cheese, soft

1 teaspoon coriander, ground

½ teaspoon rosemary, dried

3 tablespoons tomato passata

Directions:

In a bowl, mix the egg with the cheese, cream cheese, coriander and rosemary and stir well. Preheat the waffle iron over high heat, pour half of the chaffle mix, cook for 6 minutes and transfer to a plate. Repeat with the rest of the batter, divide the tomatoes, tomato passata and rosemary over the chaffles and serve.

Nutrition: calories 252, fat 4.3, fiber 2.2, carbs 5, protein 11.2

41.   Jalapeno Chaffle

Preparation time: 5 minutes

Cooking time: 10 minutes

Servings: 6

Ingredients:

2 eggs, whisked

2 cups almond milk

2 tablespoons avocado oil

½ cup cheddar, shredded

1 cup almond flour

1 tablespoon baking powder

A pinch of salt and black pepper

½ teaspoon garlic powder

2 jalapenos, minced

Directions:

In a bowl, mix the eggs with the milk, oil and the other ingredients and whisk well.

Preheat the waffle iron, pour 1/6 of the batter, cook for 8 minutes and transfer to a plate.

Repeat with the rest of the batter and serve.

Nutrition:

calories 381, fat 14, fiber 3.6, carbs 13, protein 13

42.   Green Chili Chaffle

Preparation time: 10 minutes

Cooking time: 10 minutes

Servings: 6

Ingredients:

2 eggs, whisked

1 and ½ cup almond flour

½ cup cream cheese, soft

½ cup almond milk

1 teaspoon baking soda

A pinch of salt and black k pepper

½ cup green chilies, minced

1 tablespoon chives, chopped

Directions:

In a bowl, mi the eggs with the flour, cream cheese and the other ingredients and whisk.

Preheat the waffle iron, pour 1/6 of the batter, close the waffle maker, cook for 8 minutes and transfer to a plate.

Repeat with the rest of the batter and serve.

Nutrition:

calories 265, fat 7, fiber 3, carbs 5.4, protein 6

43.   Hot Pork Chaffles

Preparation time: 10 minutes

Cooking time: 10 minutes

Servings: 4

Ingredients:

1 cup pulled pork, cooked

2 tablespoons parmesan, grated

2 eggs, whisked

2 red chilies, minced

1 cup almond milk

1 cup almond flour

2 tablespoons coconut oil, melted

1 teaspoon baking powder

Directions:

In a bowl, mix the pulled pork with the eggs, parmesan and the other ingredients and whisk well.

Heat up the waffle maker, pour ¼ of the chaffle mix, cook for 8 minutes and transfer to a plate.

Repeat with the rest of the mix and serve.

Nutrition:

calories 300, fat 13, fiber 4, carbs 7.2, protein 15

44.   Spicy Chicken Chaffles

Preparation time: 10 minutes

Cooking time: 10 minutes

Servings: 4

Ingredients:

2 eggs, whisked

1 cup rotisserie chicken, skinless, boneless and shredded

1 cup mozzarella, shredded

½ cup milk

2 teaspoons chili powder

1 teaspoon sriracha sauce

1 tablespoon chives, chopped

½ teaspoon baking powder

Directions:

In a bowl, mix the eggs with the chicken, mozzarella and the other ingredients and whisk.

Preheat the waffle maker, pour ¼ of the batter, cook for 10 minutes and transfer to a plate.

Repeat with the rest of the batter and serve.

Nutrition:

calories 320, fat 8, fiber 2, carbs 5.3, protein 12

45.   Spicy Ricotta Chaffles

Preparation time: 10 minutes

Cooking time: 10 minutes

Servings: 4

Ingredients:

2 cups coconut flour

1 and ½ cups coconut milk

2 tablespoons olive oil

A pinch of salt and black pepper

½ cup ricotta cheese

1 teaspoon baking powder

2 eggs, whisked

½ cup chives, chopped

1 red chili pepper, minced

1 jalapeno, chopped

Directions:

In a bowl, mix the flour with the milk, oil and the other ingredients and whisk well. Heat up the waffle iron, pour ¼ of the batter, cook for 10 minutes and transfer to a plate. Repeat with the rest of the chaffle mix and serve.

Nutrition:

calories 262, fat 8, fiber 2.4, carbs 3.2, protein 8

46.   Spicy Black Sesame Chaffles

Preparation time: 10 minutes

Cooking time: 10 minutes

Servings: 4

Ingredients:

2 cups almond flour

2 cups almond milk

Juice of ½ lemon

1/3 cup black sesame seeds

A pinch of salt and black pepper

2 eggs, whisked

1 teaspoon chili powder

1 teaspoon hot paprika

Directions:

In a bowl mix the almond flour with the almond milk and the other ingredients and whisk well. Heat up the waffle iron, pour ¼ of the batter and cook for 10 minutes.

Repeat with the rest of the mix and serve.

Nutrition: calories 252, fat 8, fiber 2.3, carbs 4, protein 4.5

47.   Spicy Zucchini Chaffles

Preparation time: 10 minutes

Cooking time: 8 minutes

Servings: 6

Ingredients:

1 and ½ cups almond flour

2 teaspoons baking powder

2 eggs, whisked

1 and ½ cups coconut milk

2 zucchinis, grated

1 teaspoon chili powder

1 teaspoon cayenne pepper

1 cup cheddar cheese, shredded

Directions:

In a bowl, mix the almond flour with the eggs, milk and the other ingredients and whisk well.

Preheat the waffle iron, pour 1/6 of the batter, cook the chaffle for 8 minutes and transfer to a plate.

Repeat with the rest of the batter and serve.

Nutrition:

calories 252, fat 7, fiber 2.3, carbs 5, protein 8.4

48.   Tabasco Chaffle

Preparation time: 5 minutes

Cooking time: 8 minutes

Servings: 4

Ingredients:

1 cup coconut milk

1 cup coconut flour

2 teaspoons Tabasco sauce

2 eggs, whisked

2 tablespoons ghee, melted

½ cup mozzarella, shredded

1 teaspoon cayenne pepper

1 tablespoon chives, chopped

1 tablespoon baking powder

A pinch of salt and black pepper

Directions:

In a bowl, mix the milk with the flour, Tabasco sauce and the other ingredients and whisk well. Preheat the waffle iron, pour ¼ of the batter, cook for 8 minutes and transfer to a plate. Repeat with the rest of the batter and serve.

Nutrition:

calories 301, fat 11, fiber 3.6, carbs 10, protein 8.3

49.　Green Cayenne Chaffle

Preparation time: 10 minutes

Cooking time: 10 minutes

Servings: 4

Ingredients:

1 cup coconut flour

½ cup cream cheese, soft

½ cup coconut milk

1 tablespoon chives, chopped

1 tablespoon parsley, chopped

1 green chili pepper, minced

½ teaspoon cayenne pepper

1 teaspoon baking soda

Directions:

In a bowl, mi the eggs with the cream cheese, milk and the other ingredients and whisk well.

Preheat the waffle iron, pour ¼ of the batter, close the waffle maker, cook for 10 minutes and transfer to a plate.

Repeat with the rest of the batter and serve.

Nutrition:

calories 273, fat 11.2, fiber 3, carbs 5.4, protein 6

50.   Hot Pesto Chaffles

Preparation time: 10 minutes

Cooking time: 7 minutes

Servings: 4

Ingredients:

1 cup almond milk

1 cup mozzarella, shredded

1 cup coconut flour

3 tablespoons basil pesto

1 teaspoon hot paprika

1 teaspoon chili powder

2 eggs, whisked

1 tablespoon ghee, melted

1 teaspoon baking soda

Directions:

In a bowl, mix the milk with the cheese, pesto and the other ingredients and whisk.

Heat up the waffle maker, pour ¼ of the mix, cook for 7 minutes and transfer to a plate.

Repeat with the rest of the mix and serve.

Nutrition:

calories 250, fat 13, fiber 4, carbs 7.2, protein 15

Conclusion

The ketogenic diet is one that has many important aspects and information that you need to know as someone who wants to try this diet. It is important to remember the warning that we have given you at the beginning of the book that this is not a diet that is safe and that doctors recommend you don't try it, or if you are going to attempt it remember that you shouldn't do so for longer than six months and even then never without the constant supervision of a doctor or at the very least a doctor knowing that your doing this and you following their guidelines and words exactly so that they can make sure that you are safe.

The ketogenic diet is a diet that believes that by minimizing your carbs, you will, while maximizing the good fat in your system and making sure that you're getting the protein you need, that you will be happier and healthier. In this book, we give you the information to know what this diet is all about, as well as describing the different types and areas that this diet will offer. Most people assume that there is only one way to do this, and while there is one thing that the additional options share, there are actually four different options you can choose from. Each one has it's unique benefits, and you should know about each type to learn what would be best for your body, which is why we have described them in the book for you to have the best information possible when you begin this diet for yourself.

Another big thing about this diet is that many people don't understand the importance of exercise with this diet. The best way to become healthier is to do three things for yourself. Get the right amount of sleep, eat healthily, and make sure that you get the proper amount of exercise as well for your body to work at an optimum level. As such, we explain the exercises that are the best to go with your diet to make sure that you are getting the most out of it.

For women who are on the go and have a busy lifestyle, we have provided recipes for a thirty-day meal plan so that you can make food quickly and have a great meal for your

lifestyle. They also have enough servings for you to have leftovers so that you don't have to worry about preparing in the morning. Instead, you can simply pack it up and take it with you wherever you go. This works out so much easier for so many people because they don't have to cook in the morning, and it saves a busy person a lot of time.

We also provide helpful ideas on how you can use these recipes for meals to make sure that you see how the numbers will affect you and make an impact on your day. A great example that we have explained is if you have a big breakfast that is full of the protein you need, for example, thirty grams, you've got to take note of this and be aware because if you eat too much for your dinner or another meal, you will throw your numbers out of where they are supposed to be. For those that have more time on their hands, we offer a thirty-day meal plan for you as well with all-new recipes to enjoy and tips and tricks for making them work for you in the best way.

With all of this information at your fingertips, you will be able to enjoy this diet and use it to your advantage. Another benefit that we offer? We explain routines that you can do for yourself to make this diet last longer for you and to benefit your body better as a result. Routines are very important and can be a big help to your body but also your spirit and your mind. This will help you utilize the diet better, and you will be able to improve with it as well as have it become easier for you to handle.

As many people are using this diet to their benefit, knowing your food is one of the biggest parts of this, and it becomes easier once you begin to use this in your daily life. One of the best things you can do is pay attention to the food that your eating and how it affects your body and mind. You will notice that this diet has the ability to make you sick, which isn't a good thing, and it's one of the things the doctors warn against. For this reason, it's very important to pay attention to what your eating and how your feeling at the same time. Another warning that we have said you need to pay attention to is that you will need to make sure that your ketogenic 'flu' isn't the result of something more serious. As people are being told that this is normal, this book has brought you the knowledge you need to be able to tell you why it's not.

This book has given you all the information you need to do this diet properly and to do it well. It's important to understand what you're getting into when you go into this diet, and this book will give you valuable information that you can use to your benefit and so you can avoid the problems that can come with this diet. You want to stay healthy and make sure that your body is able to do what it needs to. As with anything, we have put a strong emphasis on the fact that if anything feels wrong or unnatural, you will need to see a doctor to make sure that you are safe and that your body can handle this diet. Use the knowledge in this book to have amazing recipes and learn how to prepare amazing meals for yourself.